Turner Watercolors

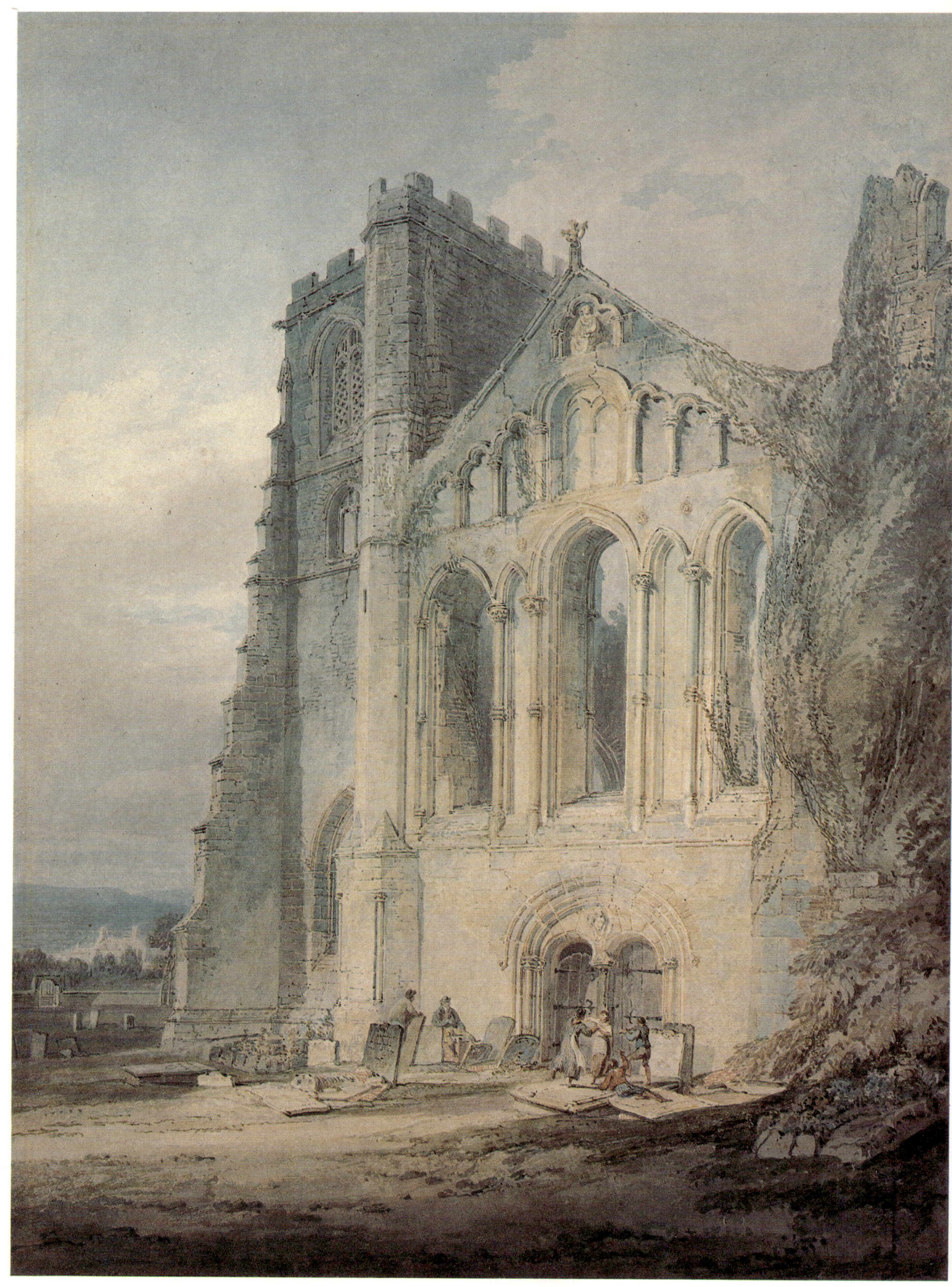

Frontispiece: Cat. No. 3, *Llandaff Cathedral, South Wales*, 1795–96

Turner Watercolors

An Exhibition of Works Loaned by
The Trustees of the British Museum

Introduction and Catalogue by Andrew Wilton

Organized and Circulated by the
International Exhibitions Foundation
1977–1978

Cover Illustration: Cat. No. 14, *Dartmouth on the River Dart*, *c.* 1823

Participating Museums

CLEVELAND MUSEUM OF ART, Cleveland, Ohio
THE DETROIT INSTITUTE OF ARTS, Detroit, Michigan
PHILADELPHIA MUSEUM OF ART, Philadelphia, Pennsylvania

Trustees of the International Exhibitions Foundation

This project is supported by a grant from the National Endowment for the Arts in Washington, D.C., a Federal agency. Support has also been received from the Federal Council on the Arts and Humanities through the Arts and Artifacts Indemnity Act. The catalogue is underwritten in part by The Andrew W. Mellon Foundation and by a grant from the British Council.

Library of Congress Card Catalogue No. 77-79293
ISBN: 0-88397-002-3
Designed and printed by Balding + Mansell, London and Wisbech

Table of Contents

Acknowledgments

The International Exhibitions Foundation is pleased to present this exhibition of outstanding Turner watercolors selected from the vast holdings of the British Museum. The great Bicentenary exhibitions of Turner's works held in London in 1975 aptly conveyed the importance of the watercolor in the development of Turner's art, and we are especially grateful for the opportunity to present some of his finest to the American public.

We wish to thank our guest director, Andrew Wilton of the Yale Center for British Art and formerly Assistant Keeper, Prints and Drawings at the British Museum, for selecting the watercolors and providing the perceptive catalogue Introduction and individual entries.

A debt of particular gratitude is owed to the Trustees of the British Museum for their generosity in making these watercolors available for tour. Mr. John Gere, Keeper of the Department of Prints and Drawings, and Mr. Reginald Williams, also of the Department of Prints and Drawings, have given valuable advice and assistance in all aspects of organization and preparation, and we are grateful for their cooperation.

Special thanks are due to Her Britannic Majesty's Ambassador, Sir Peter Ramsbotham, G.C.V.O., K.C.M.G., for graciously agreeing to sponsor the exhibition on its United States tour. Mr. Philip Lyon Roussel, O.B.E., Cultural Attaché at the British Embassy, has helped in innumerable ways.

We are most pleased to acknowledge our debt to those organizations which have rendered financial assistance for the project. The National Endowment for the Arts in Washington, D.C., a Federal Agency, has given a generous grant in support of the exhibition and catalogue. Valuable assistance has been received from the Federal Council on the Arts and Humanities through the Arts and Artifacts Indemnity Act of December 1975. We are also indebted to the Andrew W. Mellon Foundation for underwriting a portion of the costs of catalogue production, and to the British Council for its aid with catalogue and exhibition expenses.

Finally, the Foundation wishes to extend its appreciation to Mr. Guy Dawson of Balding & Mansell Ltd. for his cooperation in the production of the catalogue. I would also like to acknowledge the devoted assistance of Heidi von Kann and Stephanie Belt of the Foundation staff, who handled the necessary details of production for the exhibition and its catalogue.

Annemarie H. Pope
President
International Exhibitions Foundation

Introduction

At his death in 1851 Turner bequeathed the contents of his studio to the English nation. In addition to nearly 300 oil paintings – finished works and sketches – it included several thousand sheets of drawings and watercolors, together with nearly 300 sketchbooks. All these works on paper are now housed at the British Museum in London.

The material for this exhibition has been selected from drawings on small sheets in the Turner Bequest. It includes no examples of the large finished watercolors that Turner made for exhibition, of which a few specimens remained in his studio; likewise, there are none of the large color-studies that he frequently made. Nevertheless, even within this restriction of size, the exhibition covers the whole range of Turner's achievement in the medium of watercolor, touching his art at every point and embracing some of his most powerful public statements as well as the most intimate of his private notes.

In the early years of his career, grandeur of scale had a special importance for Turner: his development from the architectural topographer of the early 1790s to the Royal Academician and the historical painter of around 1800 entailed the steady increase in sheer size of nearly all his output. He embraced the notion of "the Sublime" – the heroic in human affairs, the overpowering in nature: his landscapes sought to convey the vastness and, often, the awfulness of natural phenomena, and for this he required to work on a scale as impressively large as possible. Not only did he shift his attention from drawing to painting: his watercolors themselves grew dramatically, while he evolved a technique that would invest them with the weight and solemnity appropriate to his new-found status and the dignity that he, like many of his fellow artists, felt should be accorded an underprivileged medium. Some of the exhibited watercolors of the late 1790s and the early 1800s are of the size of oil paintings, and Turner's preparatory work for them involved the making of a series of color studies which are often as large. But this increase in the scale of Turner's ideas can be traced as well in the smaller drawings. As early as 1792, in a study of the ruins of the burned-out Pantheon (No. 2), we can detect a broadening of vision to subsume detail in atmospheric effect that is prophetic of Turner's future preoccupations. By the middle of the decade, he could hold a balance between accurate recording and the evocation of light in a large three-dimensional atmosphere that contrasts strikingly with his work of five years before (compare Nos. 1 and 3). The actual dimensions of the sheet on which the drawing was made are not decisive: he creates his own scale by the manipulation of these broad elements.

Drawing in line underwent a parallel transformation. The precise, controlled pencil outline in which Turner was accustomed to collect the factual material for his watercolors gradually loosened to become a much more flexible and expressive instrument, though he used the pencil throughout his life to make detailed notes of buildings or views that attracted him on his journeys. In a study like that of *Dunstanborough Castle* (No. 4), which is one of a series related to an oil painting (or, less probably, to a watercolor that he made of the same subject), the large scale and wild grandeur of the Northumberland coast are evoked by the sheer vigor and power with which he sets down his motif. In this case he uses a rough toned paper which rather suggests that the drawing is preparatory for a picture. He invariably executed his large finished watercolors on smooth white paper; and indeed, with some exceptions that we shall note, he favored good quality white Whatman or similar paper for all his work in watercolor throughout his life.

He was nevertheless interested in the possibility of modifying the surface that his paper provided, and, when he visited Switzerland in 1802, prepared some of his sketchbooks with washes of gray color analogous to the preparation of a canvas before a subject is laid in. He also took with him one book of gray paper, on which he worked with strong and fluent black chalk, aided by some white chalk and sometimes by pencil as well. These monochrome studies were often developments of subjects that he had previously noted in a rapid pencil sketch (No. 5), and are frequently complete statements of a visual drama that is clearly an elaboration on simple reality: restricted not only in scale but also in medium and color, and certainly not intended as finished or "public" statements, they are nevertheless impressive evocations, complete in themselves, of the "Sublime" scenery that had become by the end of the eighteenth century the vehicle in landscape for the highest emotions. In fact, they were frequently used as the starting-points for larger watercolor drawings that are truly "finished," in the minute and detailed technique that Turner had evolved by this date. This technique consisted in the application of layer upon layer of watercolor, in broad free washes which could be punctured by blotting, rubbing, scratching or smearing with the fingers, or built up into areas of exquisite detail by means of finely controlled hatching. As the new century progressed this extraordinary technical resource – far richer than that of any other practitioner of watercolor – was developed and refined until, by about 1815, it had reached such a pitch of flexibility and precision that Turner could use it to express anything he wished.

What he wished to express was itself immensely complex. His view of the world was profound and penetrating, a perpetual eagle-eyed sharpness towards the things around him, both of man and of nature, which he forged into coherent and universal statements about life. We have only to observe the clarity and lucidity with which he captures the essence of natural detail in loving studies of trees or fish, for instance (Nos. 7 and 16), to become aware of Turner's wide-ranging sympathy and understanding. At the same time, he could reduce a design to its elements with a single clear sweep of the brush dipped in ink (No. 8), and on to such a framework he could build a structure of immense grandeur and diversity, in which a multiplicity of content finds its complete expression in every last detail (compare No. 8 with No. 15).

A direct consequence of this technical flexibility was that Turner did not need to confine himself to large-scale works in order to convey his high and intricate meaning. As early as 1812 he was beginning to concentrate all the content of a panorama into a few square inches of space; in some of the work that he produced for the engravers in the ensuing decade, he executed with the fine point of a small brush conceptions as grand as his largest paintings: the little drawing of *Dartmouth on the River Dart*, for example (No. 14), is a comprehensive account of the local economy of Dartmouth, its buildings, inhabitants and pursuits – and all presented as a serenely balanced classical harbor scene, melting in an infinitely subtle evening light.

After this period in which Turner wrestled with watercolor and subdued it completely to his will he hardly ever again needed to make large-scale works in the medium. In the early twenties he produced some – like the impressive *Grenoble Bridge* of 1824, now in the Baltimore Museum of Art; and in 1829 he recorded an experience in a snowstorm in which he himself appears, on a sheet of exceptionally large size for that date (*Messieurs les Voyageurs*,[1] British Museum, Lloyd Bequest). Thereafter, his largest watercolors are the studies that he made for finished works, preparations, sketches, broadly-planned color schemes. The final statement in almost every case is smaller and more intense; complexity of technique conveying scale and atmosphere replaces grandeur of actual size. Nothing could better illustrate this state of affairs than Turner's exercises in book-illustration in the late twenties, which continued almost throughout the thirties. Some of the later of these illustrations were conceived as full-page plates, in a regular rectangular format, not unlike those of the *Southern Coast* or *Rivers of England* series produced in the 1810s and early 1820s. But in these there is, if anything, even less concern to suit subject to format, and the tendency of so much of his work towards the panoramic often reaches an extreme of grandiose expansion in the tiny views of Edinburgh he made for Cadell's *Scott*, or of the Himalayas that appeared in White's *Views in India*. There is no essential distinction between the expressive capacity of the large watercolor and that of the small. In the vignette illustrations, however, he formulated a new response because the very shape of the design was different. It was, first of all, a circular image and not a rectangular one; and, secondly, it was not confined within a firm boundary line: the subject could be made to blend softly with the whiteness of the paper – an additional weapon in the technical armory. Turner could concentrate his ideas into an exceptionally small space, which was by nature and definition circular – vortical, compositionally intense: we must suppose that his work on the vignettes helped him to arrive at the format of several of his most individual late works, the pair of *War* and *Peace*,[2] for instance (Tate Gallery), or *Glaucus and Scylla*[3] (Kimbell Art Museum, Fort Worth). He could also use the whiteness of the paper not only, as in traditional watercolor procedure, to create light within the work, but to expand the whole image outwards into an indefinite aura of radiance. No subject embodies the idea better than that of *The Alps at Daybreak* (No. 51): it is a complete vision in miniature of the Turnerian Sublime.

Two preliminary studies, or possibly unfinished drawings, of vignette subjects (Nos. 55 and 56) present us with a remarkable demonstration of the way in which these little visions were constructed, almost from the beginning, in brilliant color. There seems to be a direct connection between the need to be interpreted by the engraver in black and white and Turner's use of bright color: as if it were only by emphasizing the essentially coloristic character of his vision that he could hope to persuade engravers to translate it adequately. We find the same process in the contemporary series of studies that Turner made for an unfinished project, illustrating the "Great Rivers of Europe," of which only the *Loire* and the *Seine* were published. Here, once again, the scale on which Turner works is small; and, unusually for him, he chooses a rather coarse paper toned either blue or gray. He employed similar small sheets of this kind of paper for his drawings at East Cowes Castle in 1827 and at Petworth some time shortly after that date (see Nos. 22 and 25); for possibly a decade, between about 1825 and 1835, it seems to have been one of his favorite methods of working to paint in bodycolor on these little, torn sheets of colored paper. As with the vignettes, the color of the "Rivers of Europe" series is often of great vividness: some of the studies are executed in schemes of brilliant scarlet, blue and green (see Nos. 36 and 37); others in clear greens and yellows, or delicate pinks, oranges and purples. In these works we can see how far Turner anticipated twentieth-century expressionism in his liberated attitude to the emotive power of color: indeed, his whole output, geared as it is to theatrical and sublime exaggerations, can be described as "expressionistic" with much greater truth than as "impressionistic."

An unusual feature of the "Rivers of Europe" drawings is that their scale and technique remain similar whether they are the roughest of exploratory sketches or the most carefully wrought finished designs for the engraver. Examples of every stage in the process are represented in this exhibition. Although none of these was actually engraved, a subject such as *Namur, with the Fortress Seen from Across the River* (No. 42) has been brought to a sufficient degree of completion to place it in the category of finished works; while the study of *Blue Hills* (No. 45) is a mere note, clearly not intended even as the basis of a final design. The view of the *Invalides from the Champ de Mars* (No. 39) on the other hand, while remaining a rough sketch, contains in itself the seeds of an elaborate motif, with the indication of a review of troops or similar exercise – a characteristic introduction of human activity that gives added significance to the subject.

Even while the small blue-paper sheets were in use, another type of drawing support was edging its way into favor with Turner: this was the modest-sized sheet of Whatman paper that he could buy in light, soft-covered books which were rollable and thus easily portable on sketching expeditions. The idea of the "roll-sketchbook" was introduced in the 1820s: before that date, sketchbooks were generally custom bound in leather or boards, often with metal clasps. Turner quickly availed himself of the new idea, and used a roll sketchbook on his first journey to collect material for the "Rivers of Europe" project in 1826 (TB CCXVIII, the *Treves and Rhine* sketchbook[4]). He continued to use similar books for the rest of his life, and some of them are still intact in the Turner Bequest. The majority, however, were dismembered at an early date, probably by Turner himself, and the drawings from them often dispersed, either directly to friends and patrons, or through his agent, Thomas Griffith. These dispersed items cover a great range of types, from studies of such completeness and self-sufficiency that they were readily enjoyed as finished works even in Turner's own time, to the vaguest and most allusive sketches. The latter type were most likely taken from the artist's studio after his death: Ruskin, among others, seems to have bought numerous examples from Turner's housekeeper, Mrs. Booth.

The portable nature of the roll sketchbooks made it possible for him to work in them out of doors, but on a scale considerably larger than that of the little pocket books he generally used when taking his visual notes. But he had always favored this size (about 9 × 11 inches) for his more elaborate sketches and color studies – the *Tabley* sketchbook No. 1 of about 1808 is of the same format (see No. 7) and so is the *Como and Venice* sketchbook of 1819 (see No. 11). He used a roll sketchbook for the rapid sketches in color that he made of the burning of the Houses of Parliament in 1834, and in the 1840s seems to have filled dozens of such books with sequence after sequence of visions (or memories?) of sea, sky, storm and sunset. These later studies occupy a place in his work that is somewhat analogous to that of the oil studies of waves, clouds and other natural phenomena that he made in large numbers in his later years. But whereas the finished oil paintings came more and more to borrow the technical characteristics of his free oil studies, the finished watercolors did not partake of a similar freedom.

There are sheets from roll sketchbooks which contain some of the most satisfying and poignant of Turner's utterances in watercolor – the *S. Giorgio Maggiore at Sunset* (No. 61) is an example; but, even if they were sold to patrons, such studies were not strictly finished works. The story of how Turner presented a set of such studies, some very highly wrought – examples here are Nos. 67 and 70 – to his agent, asking for commissions for finished drawings based upon them, is well known (see No. 67). The watercolors that he made in response to these commissions are very clearly a different kind of object from the studies from which they derive. They are larger, though not very large: usually about 12 × 18 inches; but like some of the little "Rivers of England" drawings of twenty years earlier they comprehend a vast area of landscape. Turner found in Switzerland, in the last decade of his life, a grandeur of scale and a breadth of atmosphere that he found, perhaps, nowhere else: his frequent visits to Lucerne in the early 1840s, until his health gave way, demonstrate a deep-seated sense of affinity, and the finished watercolors of Swiss subjects, together with the quantities of studies that he made, all confirm this. He sought particularly the most expansive views, the scenery that was the largest in scale: mountains and lakes, or cities seen in vast panoramas, rather than the forested slopes, gullies and waterfalls that had occupied him most on his first visit in 1802. But whereas after that first visit he made some of his biggest watercolors, now in the 1840s he could express a greater sense of vastness, of infinite air and space, on a restricted sheet of paper. We may note that his oil paintings, too, are usually smaller in size at the end of his life: the last really large canvases that he painted were some of those done in Rome in 1828 or shortly afterwards.

In general, Turner did not make watercolors as preparations for his paintings. For these, he relied on the pencil notes that he made in his smaller sketchbooks, and even these are more commonly to be associated with the finished watercolors that he did for series like the "History of Richmondshire" or the "Picturesque Views in England and Wales." A drawing like the *Landscape with a Hunt* (No. 9), although it prompts conjecture as to its relation to a known painting, cannot firmly be allotted a place in the evolution of that work. We can say only that Turner's habit of exploring a given theme in a number of sequential exercises justifies us in dating the drawing to the period of the painting, but provides no proof of a functional connection. Fortunately, the hypothesis is supported by the style of the watercolor technique. The version that he painted in oils of the *Pass of St. Gotthard* (No. 6) is a rare exception to the rule; it is closely modeled on the initial study, and adds little to the large watercolor that Turner made of the same subject. Its companion, based on another leaf from the same sketchbook, is also faithful to the sketch, but adds figures in the form of Napoleonic troops crossing the narrow Devil's Bridge, and filing along the precipitous mountain road. Likewise, one of the "Rivers of Europe" drawings, engraved for *Wanderings by the Seine* in 1834, was made the foundation of a large canvas exhibited in 1833. One or two of the Venetian studies of about 1840 were also reinterpreted as paintings. The watercolor studies of the burning of the Houses of Parliament (Nos. 47, 48) do not correspond to the compositions of the two pictures he made of the scene, but obviously played an important part in forming Turner's approach to the subject: even if he did not work, as a rule, from watercolor to oil, it is clear that throughout his career the two strands of his output were interlinked in his mind, and his experience of each played a vital part in the practice of the other. The drawing of *Whalers Boiling Blubber* (No. 73) is, however, possibly more closely connected with the picture of that title exhibited in 1846 and, indeed, seems to betray by its unusually elaborate medium a function rather different from that of the majority of the studies in pure watercolor: Turner's use of bodycolor and colored chalks has the appearance of an attempt to build up masses of contrasted tone rather as he does in the painting itself.

There is, in fact, a suggestion in Turner's later work that he was attempting in his oil paintings to achieve the same extraordinary flexibility and expressive range that he commanded in watercolor. On the whole, the late paintings do not comprehend so wide a gamut of coloristic and tonal variety, and we cannot find atmospheric evocations in oil that attain the subtlety and complexity of effect so typical of, say, the Venetian studies or the finished Swiss drawings; while, on the other hand, there are few of his oil sketches so economical or so vivid as the bare *Misty Shore with Breakwater* (No. 57) and the *Rigi: Pale Gray and Yellow* (No. 69), which is almost oriental in its understatement.

Even within the range of these small works, Turner's achievement is vast, profound, and astonishingly varied. In this catalogue, the relationship of the individual items to his work in other media and in larger format has been pointed out and, where appropriate, developed to indicate the place of the small-scale works in his total output and, incidentally, to sketch a general survey of his life's work as it is reflected in them. All TB references are to A. J. Finberg's *Inventory of the Drawings of the Turner*

Bequest, and prints are referred to by their numbers in W. G. Rawlinson's *The Engraved Work of J. M. W. Turner, R.A.* (see Bibliography). Measurements are given, height before width, in inches and millimeters. The order is chronological, though in certain cases (as with the "Rivers of Europe" drawings and the book illustrations) chronology is broken to keep related items together. Many of the dates are approximate, and in the case of groups like the sky studies of about 1825 it has been possible only to give an informed guess; the reasoning behind such guesses is stated as clearly as possible in the notes. It is to be hoped that the exhibition will draw attention particularly to the fact that the dating of Turner's work cannot be based on the assumption that he became more and more liberated from academic and topographical convention: from the beginning those conventions were his tools, and not his masters; and to the end they exercised a stimulating constraint on almost everything that he did. Likewise, he was capable of the most surprising freedom in the sketches with which he prepared for finished works at all periods of his career. Few artists have packed so much expressive significance into preparatory drawings and sketches as Turner did; but we should not lose sight of the fact that, like any other artist, he attached a particular significance and value to those fully-wrought paintings and drawings in which he gave articulate and complete expression to his most complex apprehensions of the world.

Andrew Wilton

1 The full title of the drawing is: *Messieurs les Voyageurs on Their Return from Italy (par la diligence) in a Snow Drift upon Mount Tarrar, 22nd of January, 1829*. British Museum, Lloyd Bequest, 1958-7-12-431; repr. BM, 1975, No. 147, pp. 116–17.
2 *Peace – Burial at Sea* is reproduced in Walker, 1976, frontispiece. *War. The Exile and the Rock Limpet* is Butlin and Joll, 1977, No. 400.
3 *Glaucus and Scylla*, Butlin and Joll, 1977, No. 395.
4 A page from this sketchbook is reproduced in Reynolds, 1969, p. 122.

Catalogue

I

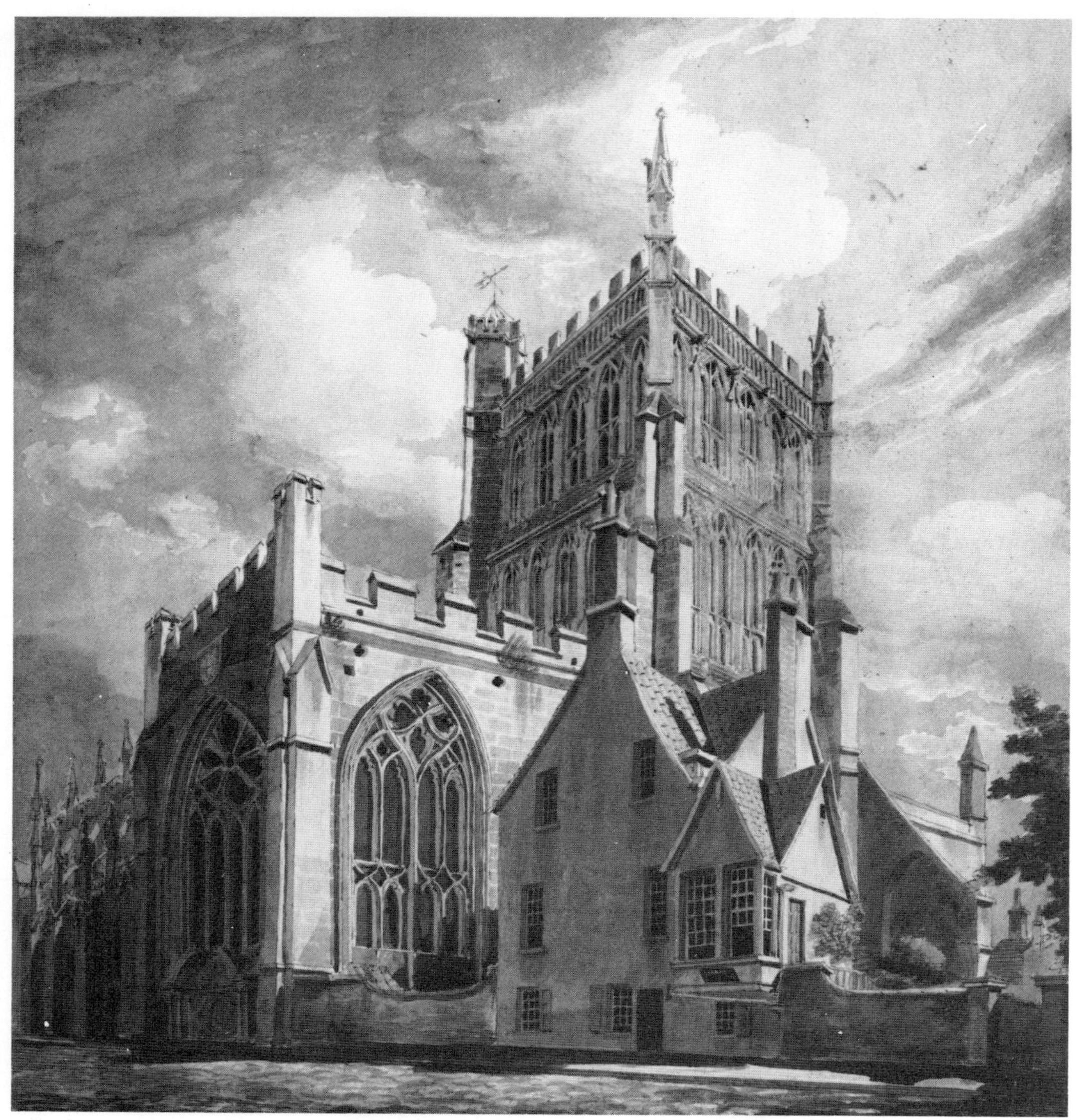

Bristol Cathedral from College Green
c. 1791

watercolor, pen and brown ink, 13¼ × 12¼ in. (337 × 312 mm.)

Inscribed *verso*: *Bristol Cathedrel* [sic]/ *from College Green/ William Turner* and *Academy/ By J Galindo Notray* [sic] *Public/ Accomptant & Translator/ Black and Gold*

TB VII-A

At the beginning of his professional career Turner worked as an assistant draftsman and print-colorer for various artists and architects; the disciplines that he learned in their studios had a marked influence on the original watercolors that he produced in the early 1790s. About the beginning of the decade, perhaps in 1789–90, he was in the workshop of Thomas Malton, Jr. (1748–1804). The first work that Turner sent to the Royal Academy, in 1790, of *The Archbishop's Palace, Lambeth*[1] (No. 644; now in the Indianapolis Museum of Art) bears strong evidence of Malton's influence, as does this drawing of Bristol Cathedral, which cannot have been made until the following year, when Turner visited Bristol for the first time, staying with John Narraway, a friend of his father's. Turner spent much of his time drawing the grand scenery of the Avon Gorge at Clifton, but he also made studies, in the *Bristol and Malmesbury Sketchbook*, TB VI, of buildings that were of particular topographical or historical interest – Bath Abbey, Malmesbury Abbey, and various country houses. Later, perhaps while he was still at Bristol, he made larger drawings based on his studies; a watercolor of *Malmesbury Abbey* appeared at the Royal Academy exhibition of 1792 (No. 436). This view of Bristol Cathedral was not exhibited, and may even have been drawn on the spot, but is evidently a finished work, and is carefully inscribed and signed on the back. The wording of the sign of a Notary Public is perhaps transcribed from the shop-board on the building in the drawing. It is characteristic of Turner to have made a careful note of such a detail; throughout his career he was to take special interest in the activities and occupations of men, and his landscapes are often conceived as comments on human life. The presentation of the cathedral here is evidently borrowed from Malton's practice of clear architectural recording, with the suggestion of drama in the steeply rising perspective that results from a deliberately low viewpoint.

1 Repr. RA, 1974–75, No. 2, p. 34.

2

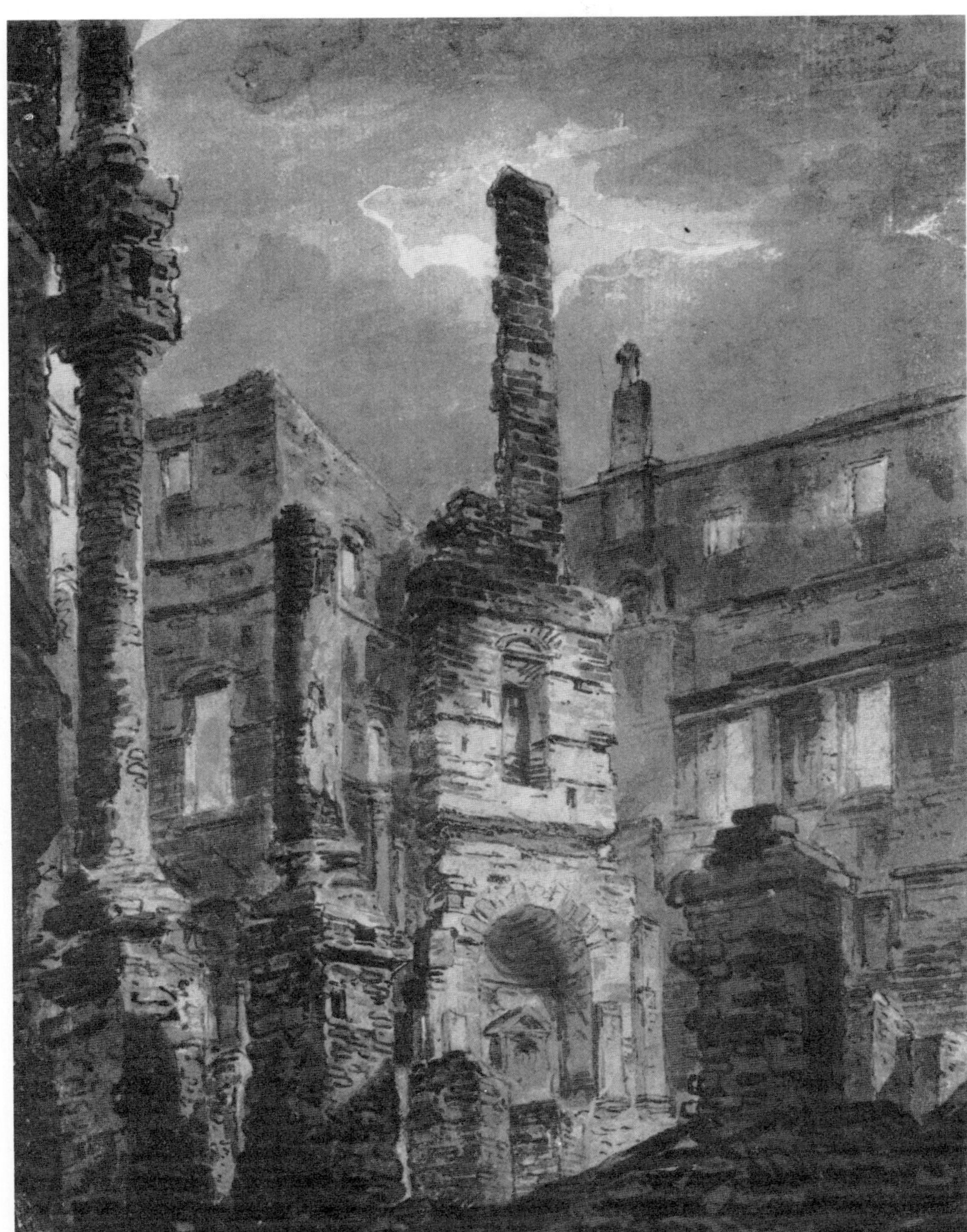

The Ruined Interior of the Pantheon, Oxford Street

1792

pencil, pen and brown ink and watercolor, $9\frac{1}{8} \times 11\frac{5}{8}$ in. (232 × 295 mm.)

TB IX-B

At the Academy exhibition of 1792 Turner showed (No. 472) a watercolor of *The Pantheon, the Morning After the Fire.*[1] This has been supposed to have been a small view of the interior of the ruined Pantheon, now untraced, which was bought by one of Turner's early employers, the architect, Thomas Hardwick. It is however very likely that the work which Turner submitted to the exhibition was the larger and very splendid drawing of the facade of the Pantheon which is now in the Turner Bequest (IX-A). This records the busy scene in Oxford Street in the early morning of the 14th January, 1792, just after the concert hall had been gutted; it presents a poetic contrast between the crowds of onlookers, early passers-by and firemen with their engine, and the ruined building, covered with icicles and catching the pink light of the sun. The subject is a striking demonstration of Turner's interest both in the human and in the atmospheric aspects of his subjects. This study of the interior illustrates, as John Gage has pointed out, (*Colour in Turner*, 1969, p.23) the extent to which already Turner had increased the expressive and tonal range of watercolor in his search after greater atmospheric subtlety. Here, and in another study of an "interior," the *Interior of the Ruins of St. Martin's Priory, Dover* (Victoria and Albert Museum) of the same year, Turner anticipates the rich effects that he was to obtain in the watercolors influenced by his first exercises in oil painting – for instance the *Trancept of Ewenny Priory, Glamorganshire,*[2] (National Museum of Wales, Cardiff) of 1796.

1 Repr. Herrmann, 1975, pl. 9.

2 Repr. Herrmann, 1975, pl. 19.

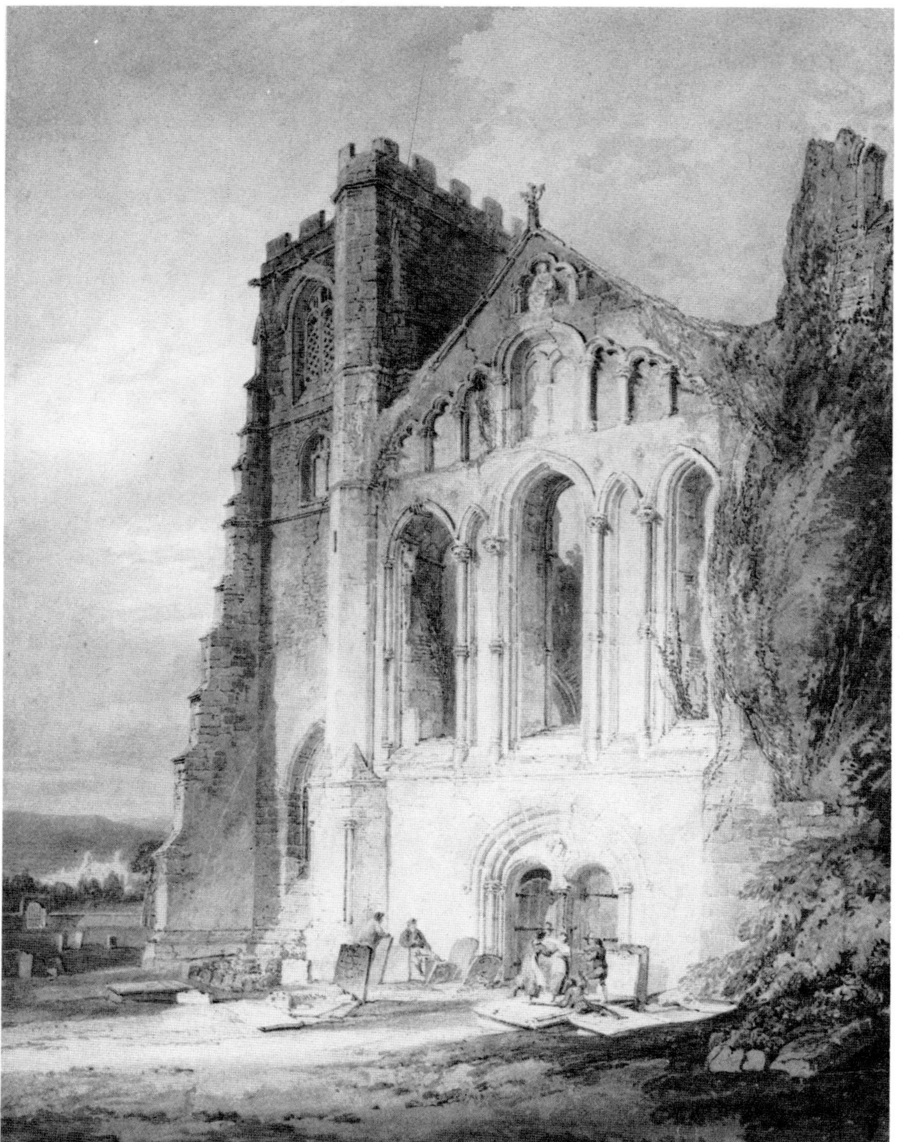

3

Llandaff Cathedral, South Wales

pencil and watercolor,
14 × $10\frac{1}{8}$ in.
(357 × 258 mm.)

TB XXVIII-A

By the middle of the decade Turner had begun to travel widely in search of picturesque or antiquarian subject matter. An outline pencil drawing of Llandaff Cathedral, made on the spot in 1795 in the *South Wales* sketchbook (TB XXVI, f. 4), was used as the basis for this watercolor. The words *Dr. Mathews* are inscribed on the back of the sheet, perhaps indicating that it was drawn for a commission; it remained, however, in Turner's studio. This is probably the drawing shown at the Royal Academy exhibition of 1796 (No. 701). It is typical of the finished topographical watercolors that Turner was making at about the time when he first began the work in oil: his painting of *Fishermen at Sea*[1] (Tate Gallery, 1585) was No. 305 in the same exhibition. That picture is concerned with the effects of moonlight, of candlelight, and the movement of the sea – an altogether more ambitious and grandiose conception than this drawing, which is itself ample evidence of Turner's need to explore new ground: it is a work of the same type as the early *Bristol Cathedral* (No. 1) and shows to what heights of poetic subtlety Turner had brought the topographical form. In technique it owes much to the example of Edward Dayes (1763–1804), the foremost topographical watercolorist of the time, but in his understanding of texture, atmosphere and light Turner is already speaking a different language. The vividness with which he presents the variegated and crumbling masonry of the cathedral is like that of Turner's exact contemporary, Thomas Girtin (1775–1802), who made very similar drawings of buildings at this period; but whereas Girtin used a rough, slightly gray or buff paper, Turner was content to work on smooth white Whatman, and laid much stress on the "finished" quality of his watercolor, lavishing great care on details such as the figures; his invention of the group of young people dancing to a fiddler on one of the tombstones is beautifully executed and an unobtrusive but pertinent comment on the whole subject.

1 Repr. Herrmann, 1975, pl. 18.

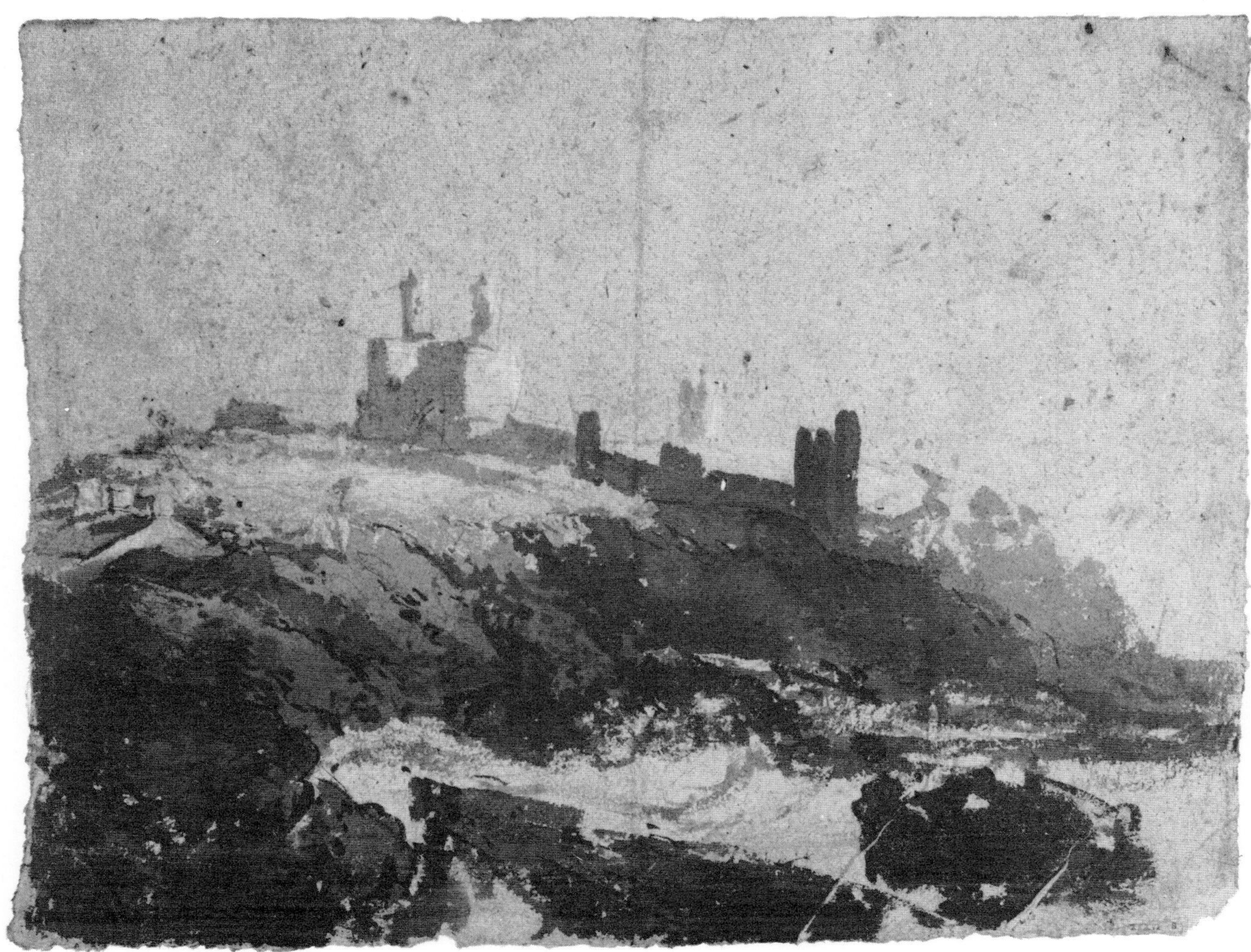

4 **Dunstanborough Castle** *c.* 1797

pencil, gray wash and white bodycolor on buff paper, $10\frac{1}{2} \times 13\frac{1}{4}$ in. (265 × 338 mm.)

TB XXXVI-S

Turner continued to work as he had always done on his travels, making careful outline drawings in pencil in his notebooks, and occasionally adding watercolor to them to experiment with particular effects. But once he had begun to paint in oil his attitude to finished watercolor changed and he began to make sequences of preparatory studies, usually in color alone, in order to establish the formal basis of tonal and chromatic relationships on which the complex final work would be founded. In the case of Dunstanborough Castle, Turner made both a watercolor (Private Collection, UK) and an oil painting (Dunedin Public Art Gallery, New Zealand),[1] and this study, together with a similar one (TB XXXIII-S) which employs watercolor as well as black ink and bodycolor, may have been used for either. The picture was shown at the RA in 1798 (No. 322); the exact date of the watercolor has not been determined. At any rate, it is evident that in this study Turner's preoccupation is with the evocation of the scale and mood of his "Sublime" subject – broad effects of tone, enhanced by the freedom of handling and the roughness of the paper, take precedence over delicacies of coloring. Turner used the same motif again, many years later, in his watercolor of Dunstanborough for the series of *Picturesque Views in England and Wales*, executed in about 1828 (City Art Gallery, Manchester).

1 Butlin and Joll, 1977, No. 32.

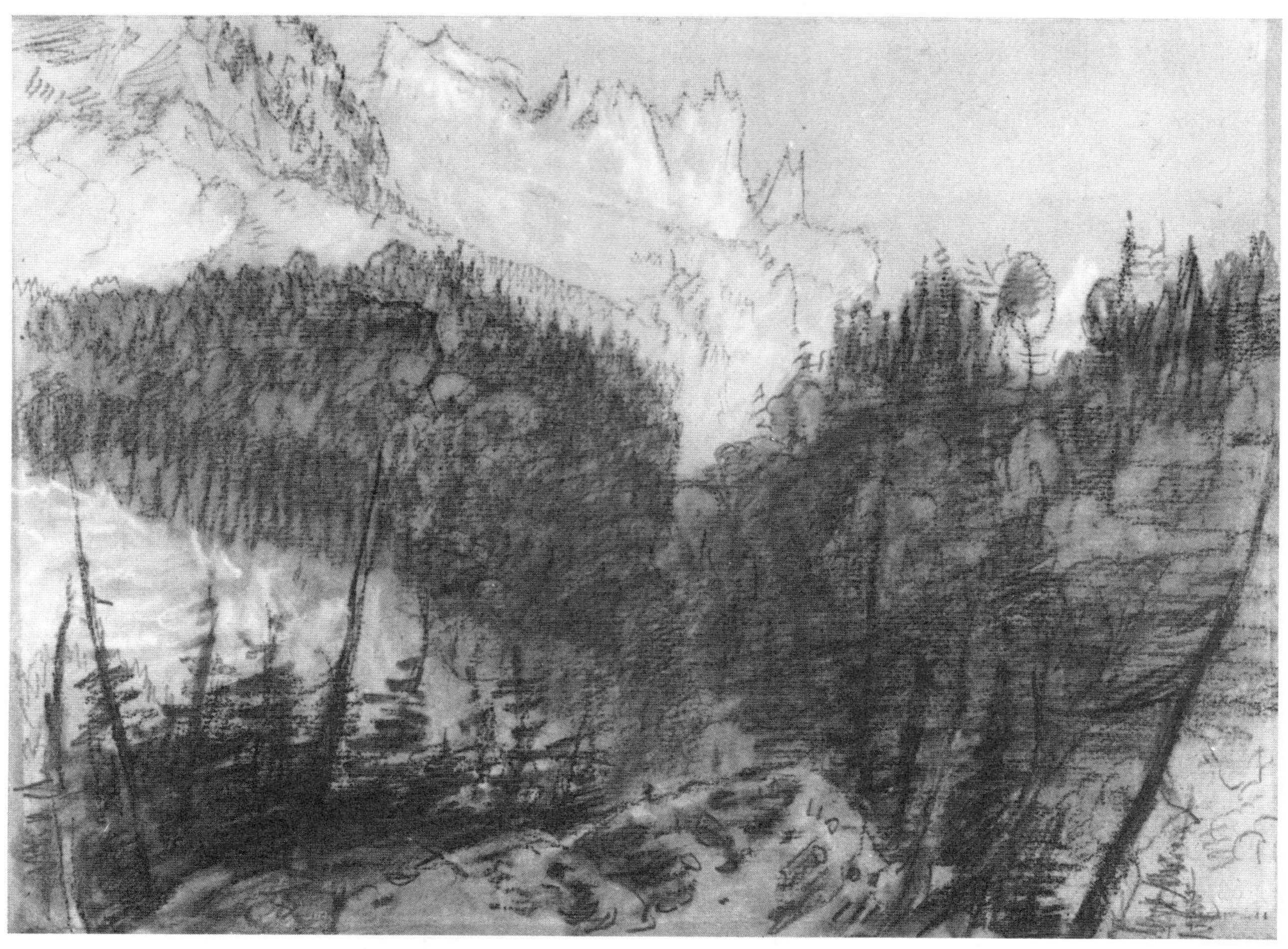

5 **Rosenlaui**

pencil, black and white chalks on gray paper (faded), $8\frac{1}{4} \times 11$ in. (210 × 281 mm.)

TB LXXIV-44

Turner's first foreign tour, made possible by the Treaty of Amiens of 1802, took him to the pre-eminently "Sublime" scenery of Switzerland, and through France, with a prolonged visit to the collections of the Louvre. The *Grenoble* sketchbook, from which this sheet comes, contains drawings made in black and white chalks on gray paper, without color. Many of them are powerful evocations of the Swiss scenery through which Turner journeyed during his tour, but in spite of their breadth of handling they are not necessarily direct records: this example is in fact worked up from a very slight outline study which occurs in another of the notebooks used on the tour, the *Rhine, Strassburg and Oxford* book, TB LXXVII-f. 29. It thus marks an additional intermediate stage between the first note of a subject and the execution of a finished watercolor. In this case, no such final version is known; an example of a design which exists in all three stages is *The Castle of Ringgenburg* (Taft Museum, Cincinnati). Turner's original sketch of *Rosenlaui*, TB LXXII-29, did not contain the ragged stumps of pine trees which render the foreground of this version so dramatically in keeping with the grandeur of the distant glaciers and peaks.

6

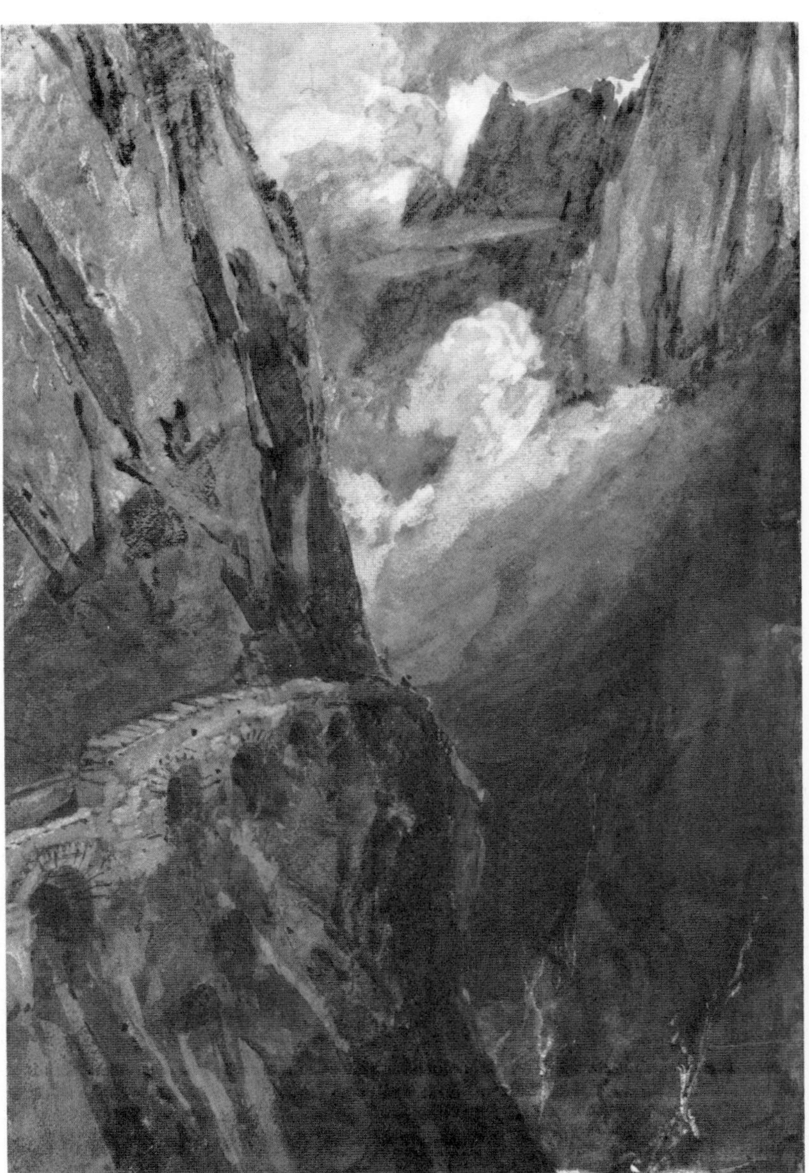

The Pass of St. Gotthard
1802

pencil, watercolor and scraping-out on white paper prepared with a gray wash, $18\frac{1}{2} \times 12\frac{3}{8}$ in. (470 × 315 mm.)

TB LXXV-33

One of the sheets of Turner's Swiss sketchbook *St. Gotthard and Mont Blanc*, in which he made many of his loveliest notes of Swiss scenery. Although some are executed in the monochrome medium of the *Grenoble* book (see No. 5), others, like this one, are worked up in subdued color to give a powerful impression of the impact on the young Turner of his first experience of the Alps. Whereas on his later visits to Switzerland he was to concentrate almost exclusively on views of great breadth, a large proportion of these early subjects are concerned with the claustrophobic rather than the expansive aspect of mountain landscape – a typically eighteenth-century preoccupation in which fear predominates over a more Romantic ecstasy. On his return to England Turner made a very large watercolor of this scene, which was one of about twenty Swiss watercolors bought from him during the next decade or so, by his friend and patron Walter Fawkes, of Farnley Hall, near Leeds in Yorkshire. The finished version (Abbott Hall Art Gallery, Kendal[1]) measures some 38 by 27 inches, and makes use of its very large size to emphasize the scale of the cliffs and the horror of the chasm. In reality, the proportions of the gorge are considerably less dramatic: this is a striking early instance of Turner's readiness to exaggerate the facts of nature in order to obtain pictorial grandeur, the *frisson* that accompanies the experience of the "Sublime." In this, his aims were precisely the reverse of those of Constable (1776–1837), who was concerned to recreate his feelings in front of a milder landscape without reference to preconceptions about the necessity for exalted emotion in serious art. A study similar to this in the same book (f. 34) shows the Devil's Bridge on which Turner stood to take this view. The two drawings were used as the bases of a pair of oil paintings; that developed from the present subject is now in the City Art Gallery, Birmingham; the other was on the London Art Market in 1977.[2]

1 Repr. Russell and Wilton, 1976, p. 61.

2 Butlin and Joll, 1977, Nos. 146, 147.

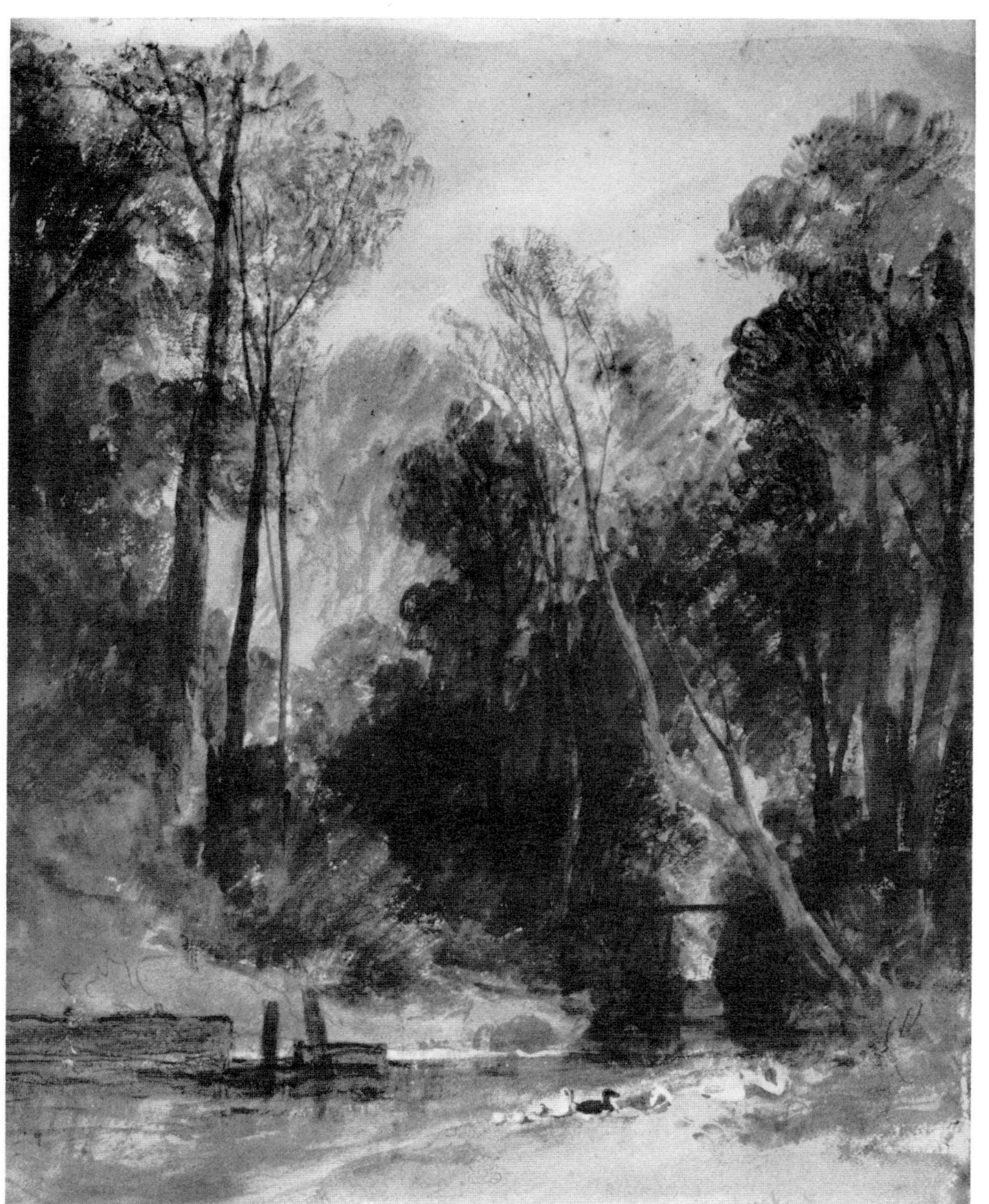

7

A Stream with Tall Trees
?1808

pencil and watercolor
$11\frac{3}{8} \times 9$ in.
(289 × 229 mm.)
Inscribed lower right: *ducks*

TB CXXI-L

After his return from the Continent Turner set to work on an ambitious program of grand pictures, inspired by the old masters he had seen in the Louvre, and of watercolors depicting the "Sublime" scenery of Switzerland (see No. 6); all of which activity was consistent with his precocious success at the Academy, of which he had been elected a full member in 1802. Throughout his life Turner laid great stress on the Academic nature of his art – on its relation to the masters of the past and on the importance of grand conceptions: unlike most of the artists who pursued that doctrine, Turner did not divorce himself from nature, but based all his "public" works on a painstaking study of the real world in all its manifestations. In about 1805 he rented a house by the Thames at Isleworth, and, during the period in which he was occupied on his great exhibition pieces, devoted much time to the quiet study of the scenery of the Thames. He seems to have worked direct from nature on to panels or canvas in oil, and he filled a sketchbook, TB XCV, with beautiful watercolor views which have all the freshness and delight in English rural scenery that we associate with Constable. This sheet is similar to that group in its mood and technique, but its dimensions are smaller than those of the sketchbook in question, which was probably in use about 1805–6. It has been suggested (by Finberg, *Inventory*, vol. I, p. 333) that the drawing belongs to the *Tabley no. I* book (TB CIII) which Turner used on his visit in 1808 to Sir John Leicester, an early patron; if so it was presumably done a little later than the Thames drawings and perhaps shows a scene at or near Tabley in Cheshire, where Leicester lived.

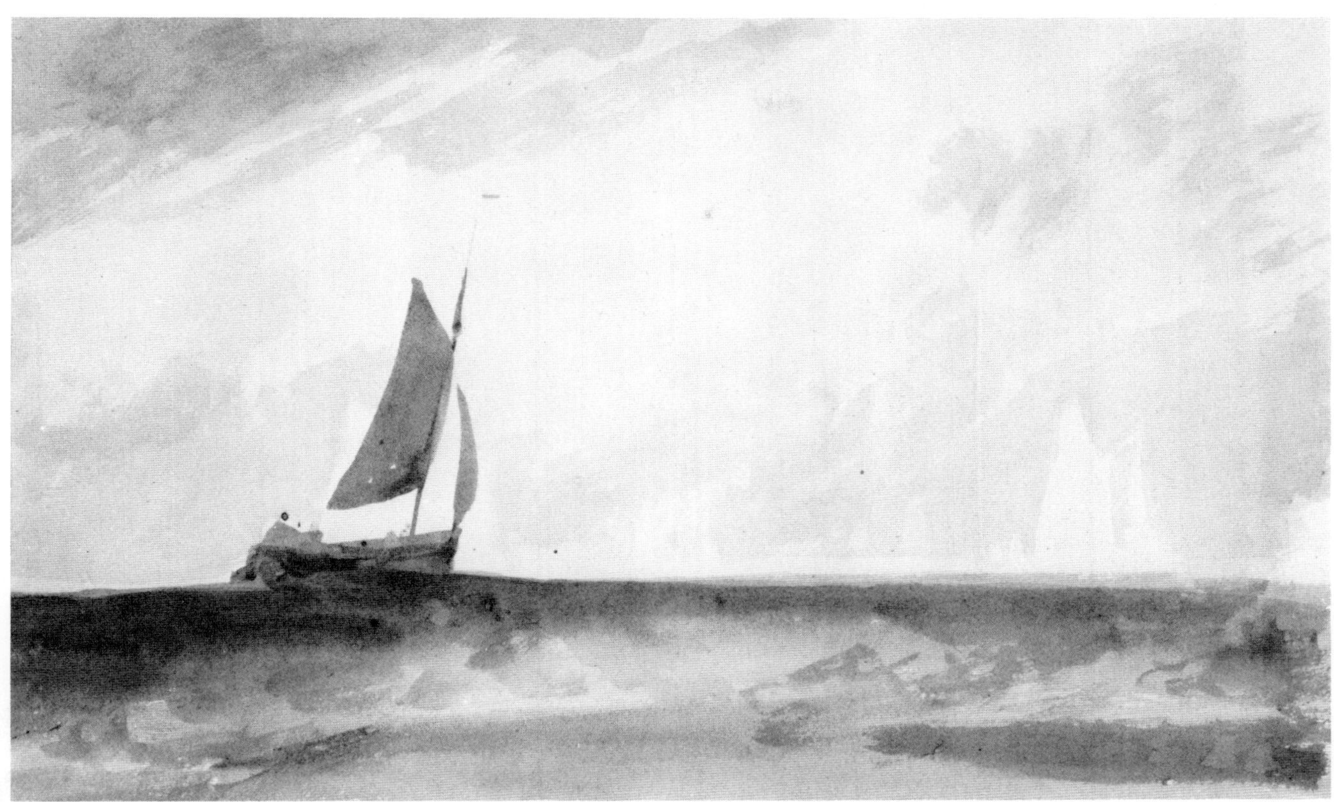

8 **Bligh Sands** *c.* 1809

brush and brown ink, $9\frac{1}{16} \times 14$ in. (230 × 356 mm.)

TB CXX-Q

In 1806 Turner began work on his *Liber Studiorum*, which was to be an extended series of plates illustrating his own work in all its varying aspects. He modeled it on Claude's *Liber Veritatis* (now in the British Museum), which had been published in the 1770s by John Boydell as a set of mezzotints with etched outlines, intended to reproduce Claude's own pen and brown wash drawings of his compositions. Turner adopted the same medium, and when preparing his designs for the *Liber Studiorum* worked largely in pen and brown ink with brown wash. In addition to the finished designs, most of which were published between 1807 and 1819, he made many preliminary studies; this is one of them which was never actually used. It is based on the painting of *Fishing Upon the Blythe-sand, Tide Setting In*,[1] which Turner showed in his own gallery in Harley Street in 1809, and exhibited again at the Royal Academy in 1815 (where it was called *Bligh Sand, Near Sheerness: Fishing Boats Trawling* – see R.A. 1974–75, No. 155). This was one of the group of marine canvases that he produced during the first decade of the century, under the influence of the Dutch artists, Ruysdael, van de Velde, van de Capelle and Backhuysen, whom he had studied in the Louvre in 1802 and in English collections. Here he has reduced the whole design to a scheme of broad tones focused on the sharp contrast of the two sails to the left; it is characteristic of Turner's method of establishing an overall unity in his designs before proceeding to break up and diversify them with detail.

1 Repr. RA, 1974–75, No. 155, p. 74.

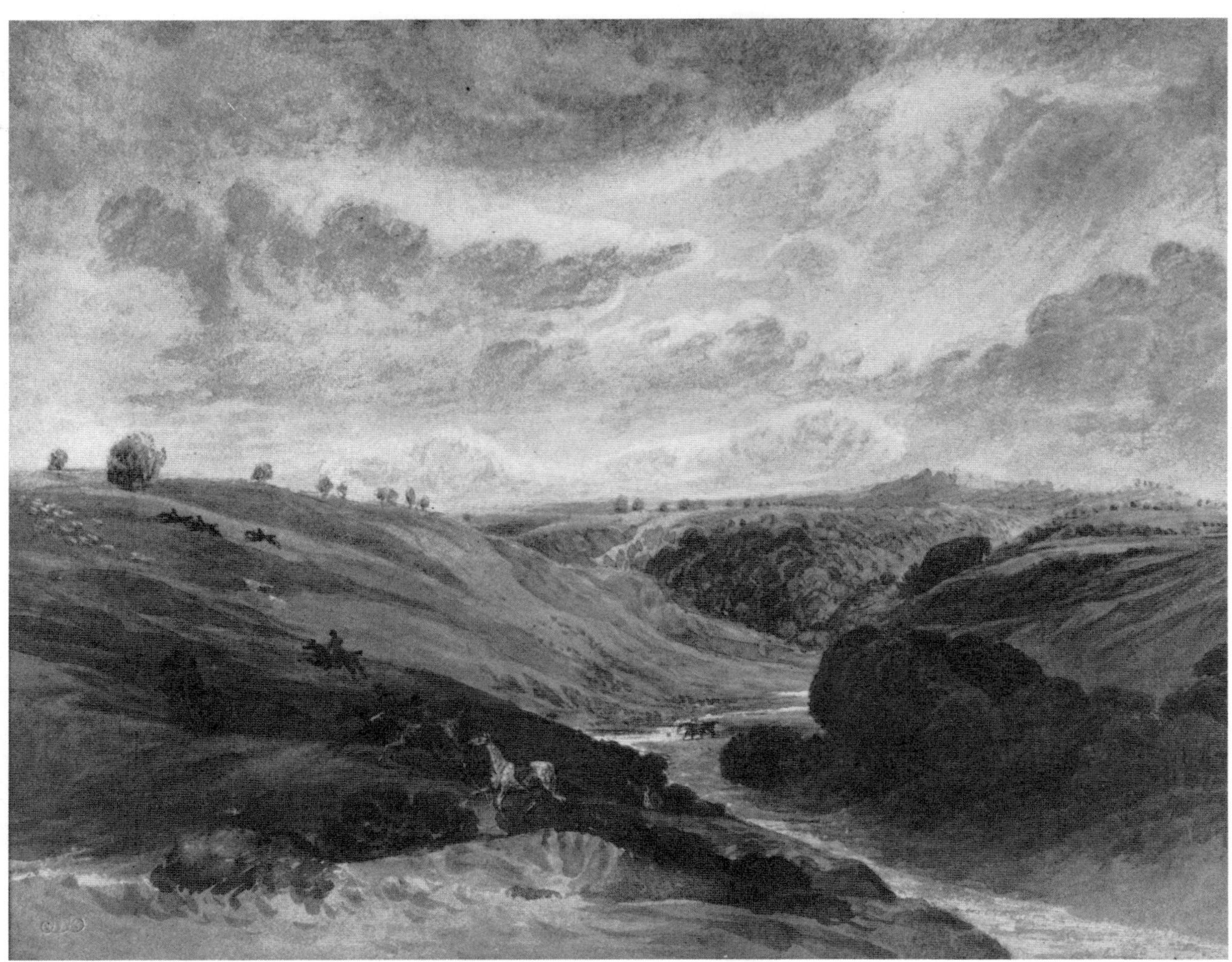

9 **Landscape with a Hunt** ?1817

watercolor over pencil, $7\frac{1}{2} \times 9\frac{1}{2}$ in. (192 × 243 mm.)

TB CXXI-Q

This unusual little drawing seems to have a thematic connection with the painting of Raby Castle,[1] which Turner executed for Lord Darlington and showed at the Royal Academy in 1818 (No. 129). The picture is now in the Walters Art Gallery, Baltimore, and is the most magnificent of the "house portraits" that Turner painted, as an extension of his old practice as a topographical draftsman. The foreground of the painting is occupied by a hunt similar to the one in this drawing. The broad sweep of the Durham landscape, noted by Turner in the *Raby* sketchbook (TB CLVI) when he stayed with Lord Darlington on his return from a tour along the Rhine in the Autumn of 1817, is not unlike the rolling green countryside that we see here, though the scene is traditionally identified as the Vale of Pickering, Yorkshire (see Finberg, *Inventory*, vol. I, p. 334). Technically, the drawing can be related to a group of larger house-portraits in watercolors that Turner was engaged on at about the same time – the views in Sussex, drawn for John Fuller, of Rose Hill; these included views of the grounds at Rose Hill and of *The Vale of Ashburnham* and *The Vale of Heathfield* (British Museum, Salting Bequest, 1910-2-12-272, 273),[2] in which Turner's mature watercolor technique evokes breathtaking panoramas of sunlit countryside fading into a hazy distance. In particular, the *Landscape with a Hunt* shows his use of delicate marbled effects to create the texture and movement of a cloudy sky.

1 Repr. Reynolds, 1969, p. 107.

2 *The Vale of Ashburnham* and *The Vale of Heathfield* are reproduced in BM, 1975, Nos. 45 and 46, pp. 48, 92–93.

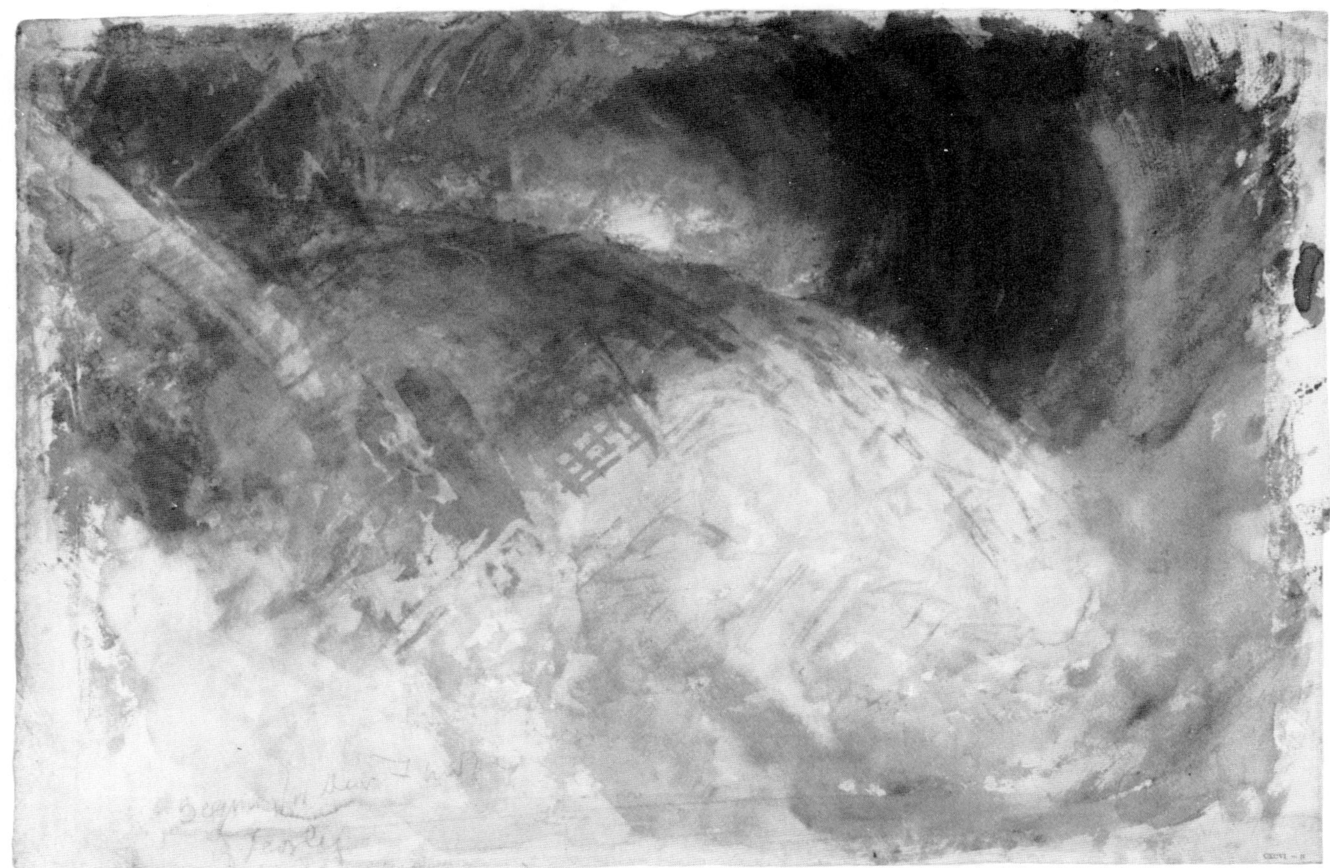

10 **Study for "The Loss of a Man o' War"** *c.* 1817

watercolor, $12\frac{3}{16} \times 18\frac{1}{8}$ in. (310 × 460 mm.)

inscribed, lower left: *Begun for Dear Fawkes of Farnley*

TB CXCVI-N

Turner made a finished watercolor of this subject in about 1818; it was bought by Walter Fawkes and is now in an English private collection. It is possible that this sheet is a rapid reminiscence of the composition, made after Fawkes's death in 1825, to which the MS comment seems to allude; but it is more likely that the drawing itself was preparatory for the watercolor and was merely annotated later. The general style of execution, and the coloring, are close to other studies of about 1817; TB CXCVI-H may have been drawn at the same time, while another, TB CXCVI-F, is related to Turner's design of *The Mew-Stone, Plymouth Sound*[1] which was engraved in 1816 as one of the plates for Cooke's *Picturesque Views of the Southern Coast of England*, and adapted for use in the *Little Liber Studiorum* in about 1825 (see No. 17). In this powerful and dramatic composition Turner may have been concerned to create a pendant to the famous *First Rate Taking in Stores* (Cecil Higgins Art Gallery, Bedford, England[2]), which he drew for Fawkes in 1818, apparently in response to Fawkes's suggestion that he make "a drawing of the ordinary dimensions that will give some idea of the size of a man of war." The *First Rate* shows the huge hull of the ship looming high on the right border of the drawing, and seen from a very low viewpoint. In the *Loss of a Man o' War* Turner tackles the same theme, that of the scale of a big ship, in a totally different way, filling the sheet with the upturned deck, which is strewn with human figures. Yet another watercolor of this period which treats similarly of a marine subject, is the *Man of War, Making a Signal for a Pilot off the Tagus*, now in the City Art Galleries, Sheffield, England. This was also owned by Fawkes, and the three subjects seem to form a "suite."

1 *The Mew-Stone at the Entrance of Plymouth Sound, Devonshire* engraved by W. B. Cooke, 1816, R.97.

2 Repr. Butlin, 1962, pl. 8.

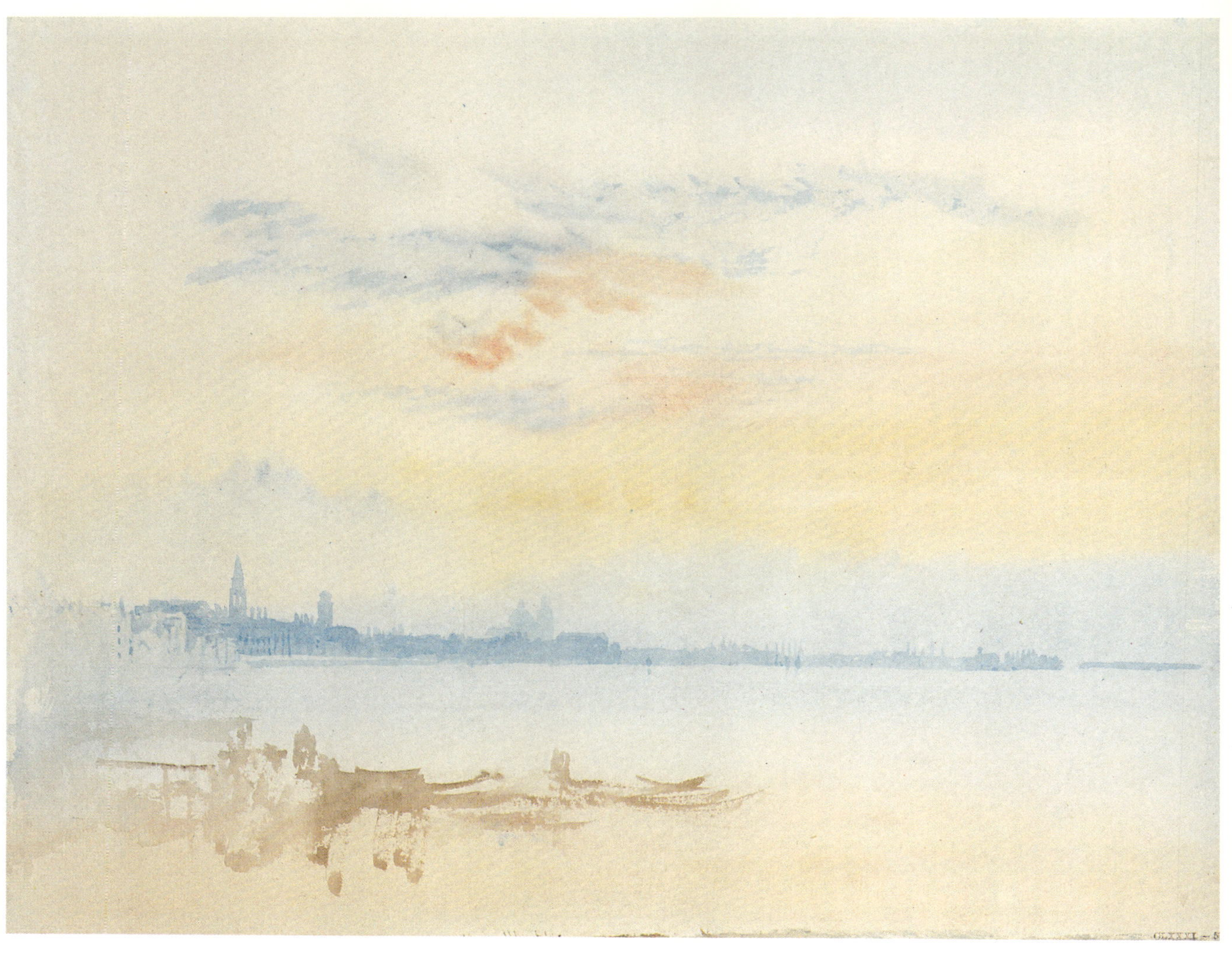

11 **Venice: Looking East from the Giudecca; Sunrise** 1819
watercolor, $8\frac{3}{4} \times 11\frac{1}{4}$ in. (222 × 287 mm.)
TB CLXXXI-5

Turner's visit to Italy in 1819 was the fulfillment of an old dream; the art and landscape of the country had occupied him in many of his most important works since before the turn of the century. His response to the new stimulus was recorded mainly in a host of pencil drawings of the buildings and antiquities that he saw in Venice, Rome and Naples, and in the towns and countryside on his intervening routes. He also made a number of color studies, some of which appear to have been done on the spot in the open air, a process which was perhaps for him a slightly abnormal one. Some of these studies are as carefully prepared and elaborately wrought as the Swiss sketches in the *St. Gotthard and Mont Blanc* book of 1802 (see No. 6); these are to be found in the books that Turner labeled *Rome C. Studies* and *Naples: Rome C. Studies* (TB CLXXXIX and CLXXXVII; see No. 12). Others have the appearance of having been dashed off instinctively as a kind of ecstatic greeting to the light and color of the Mediterranean climate. In his *Como and Venice* sketchbook (TB CLXXXI) he made two exquisite, pearly studies of Lake Como with the sunlight streaming across its mountainous banks, and four startlingly fresh notes of morning-light effects at Venice. This is the most economical and understated of the group, yet it conjures up the breadth and splendor of the scene with unparalleled clarity. Turner made a number of finished watercolors of Italian subjects for Walter Fawkes on his return to England, including one of the *Rialto*[1] (now in the collection of Dr. and Mrs. Kurt Pantzer, Indianapolis) and one of *Venice from Fusina* (in a UK private collection). An enormous canvas of the Grand Canal, seen from beneath the arch of the Rialto Bridge, was planned but remained in a very incomplete state (Tate Gallery, 5543). In practice, Turner seems to have had difficulty in giving full public expression to his response to Italy: the experience was perhaps too overwhelming, too fraught with significance for him. It was many years before he was able to draw creatively on the inspiration that Venice provided.

1 Repr. Berkeley, 1975, No. 17, p. 99.

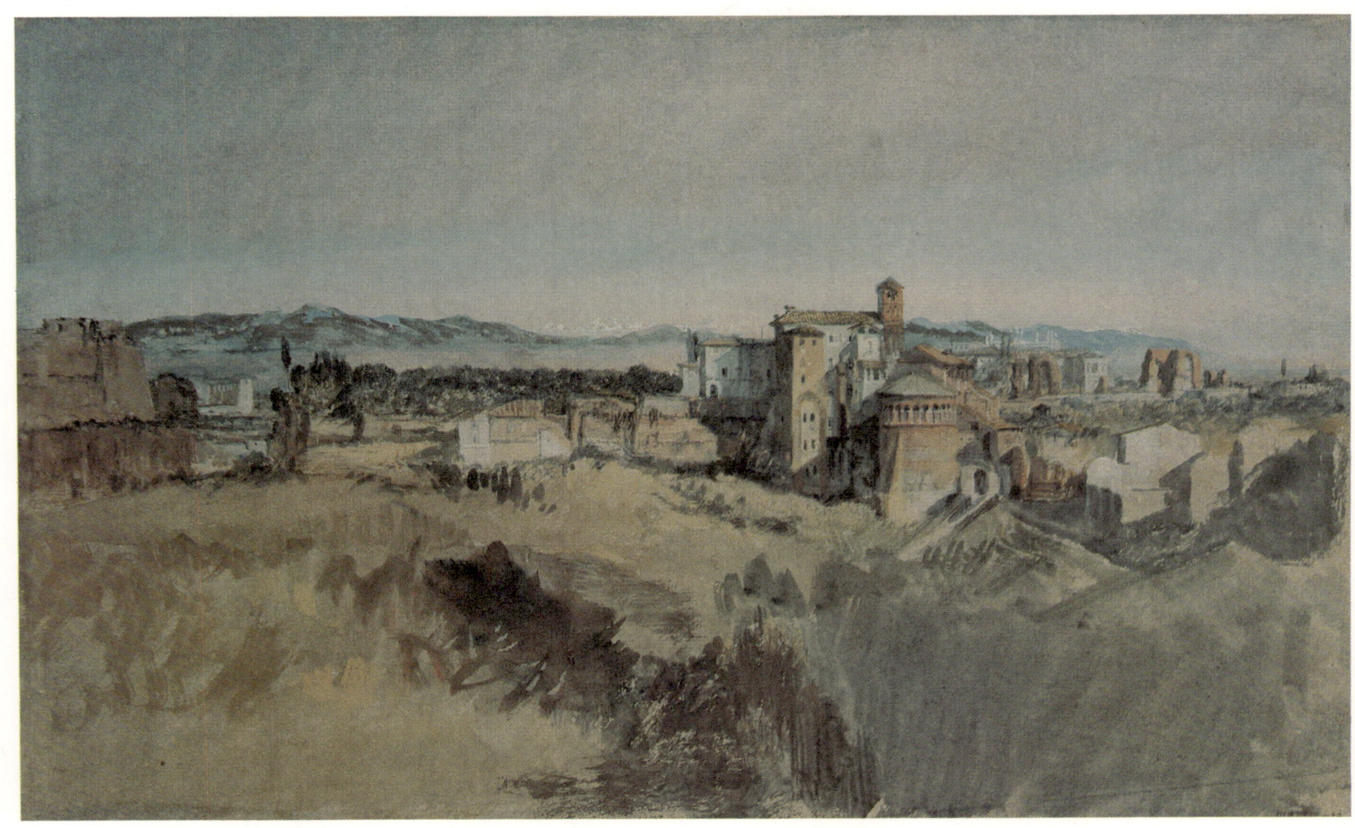

12 **Rome: The Church of SS. Giovanni e Paolo** 1819

watercolor and bodycolor on white paper prepared with a gray wash, $9\frac{1}{16} \times 14\frac{1}{2}$ in. (230 × 367 mm.)

TB CLXXXIX-39

The book from which this sheet comes was labeled by Turner: *Rome: C. Studies* and it has been presumed that "C." stands for "color," for the majority of the drawings in it are at least partially colored, and many are complete compositions in color. The same is true of the *Naples: Rome C. Studies* book (see No. 13). Nevertheless, Turner prepared no less than four of his Italian sketchbooks with the same ground of gray wash that he had employed in Switzerland in 1802, and this may be a hint that, while, as we have seen (No. 11), he was eager to catch at any new impression, he also anticipated making grand subjects using the sonorous tonal gamut of his early "Sublime" work. In practice, he often used the prepared sheets for records which, like this one, are more concerned with the loving delineation of minute detail than with the expression of general effects. It is possible that, in his handling of subjects such as this, he had in mind the delicate and meticulous work of German artists in Rome at the time – men like Georg Dillis and Josef Anton Koch. But his instinctive response to climate and atmosphere made it impossible for him to produce a "camera obscura" account of what he saw, and these Roman studies are radiant with his understanding of the quality of Italian light on Italian buildings.

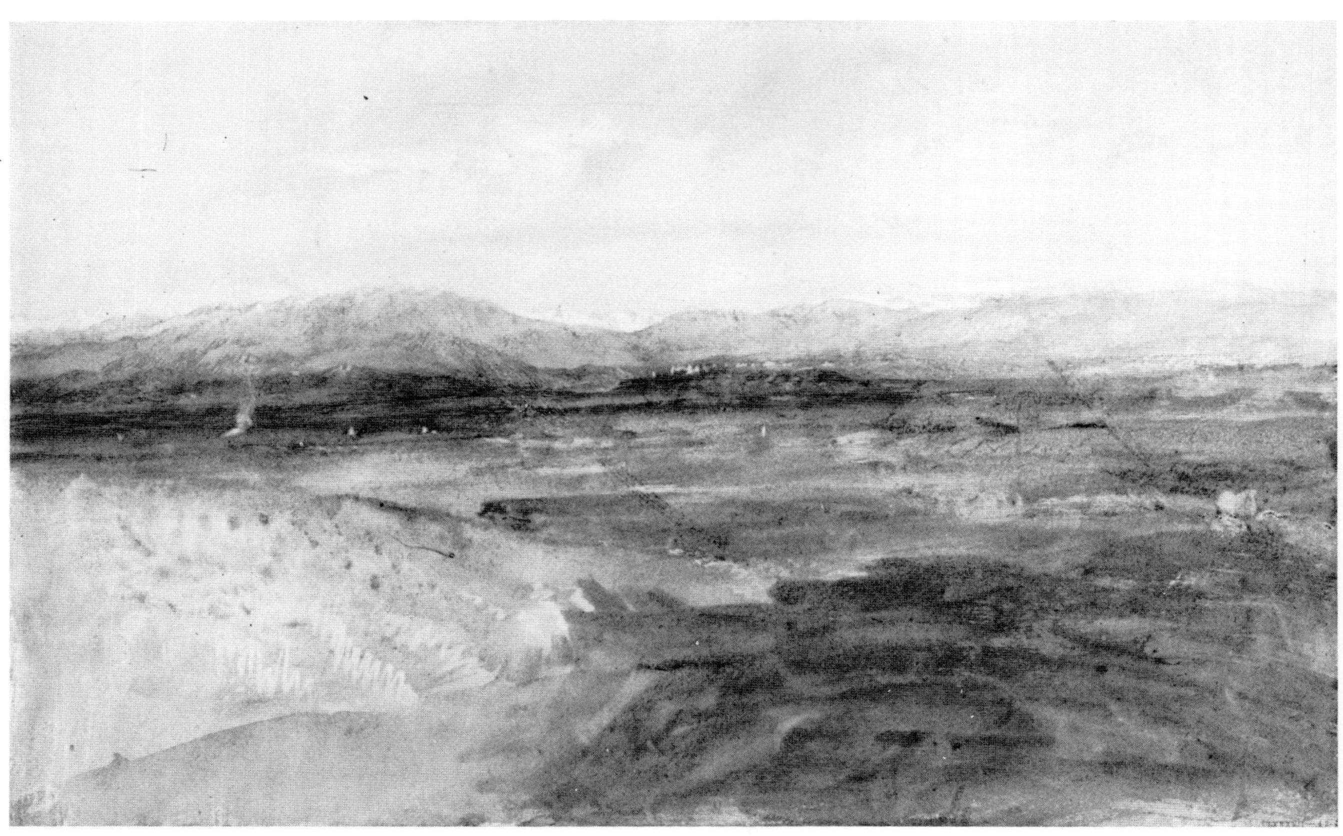

13 **A View Across the Roman Campagna** 1819

watercolor, 10 × 15$\frac{7}{8}$ in. (255 × 404 mm.)

TB CLXXXVII-42

This is a sheet from the *Naples: Rome C. Studies* sketchbook (see No. 12). The handling of watercolor in this drawing should be compared with that of No. 7, which represents Turner's style of recording directly from nature in the previous decade. There is considerable use of scraping-out with the end of the brush, and other ways of manipulating the pigment. But Turner had practised technical tricks of this kind since before 1800 – indeed, almost as soon as his work in oil began, he seems to have been aware of new possibilities in watercolor and to have applied them imaginatively, both in preliminary studies and in his finished watercolors. The principal development is in the matter of color, which underwent considerable modification under the impact of Turner's Italian experience. This is especially noticeable in a sketchbook, the *Skies* book,[1] TB CLVIII, which has hitherto been considered to belong to about the year 1818 (see R.A. 1974–75, No. 177), but which may well have been used in Italy: one of its long sequence of studies of skies seems to have been made in Italy (f. 42) and if this is so, it is likely that the others were as well. In this group of rapid color sketches we can see Turner responding with new intensity and persistence to effects of light, which also affects his treatment of the shimmering plain of the Campagna in this drawing.

1 A page from the *Skies* sketchbook is reproduced in Butlin, 1962, pl. 7.

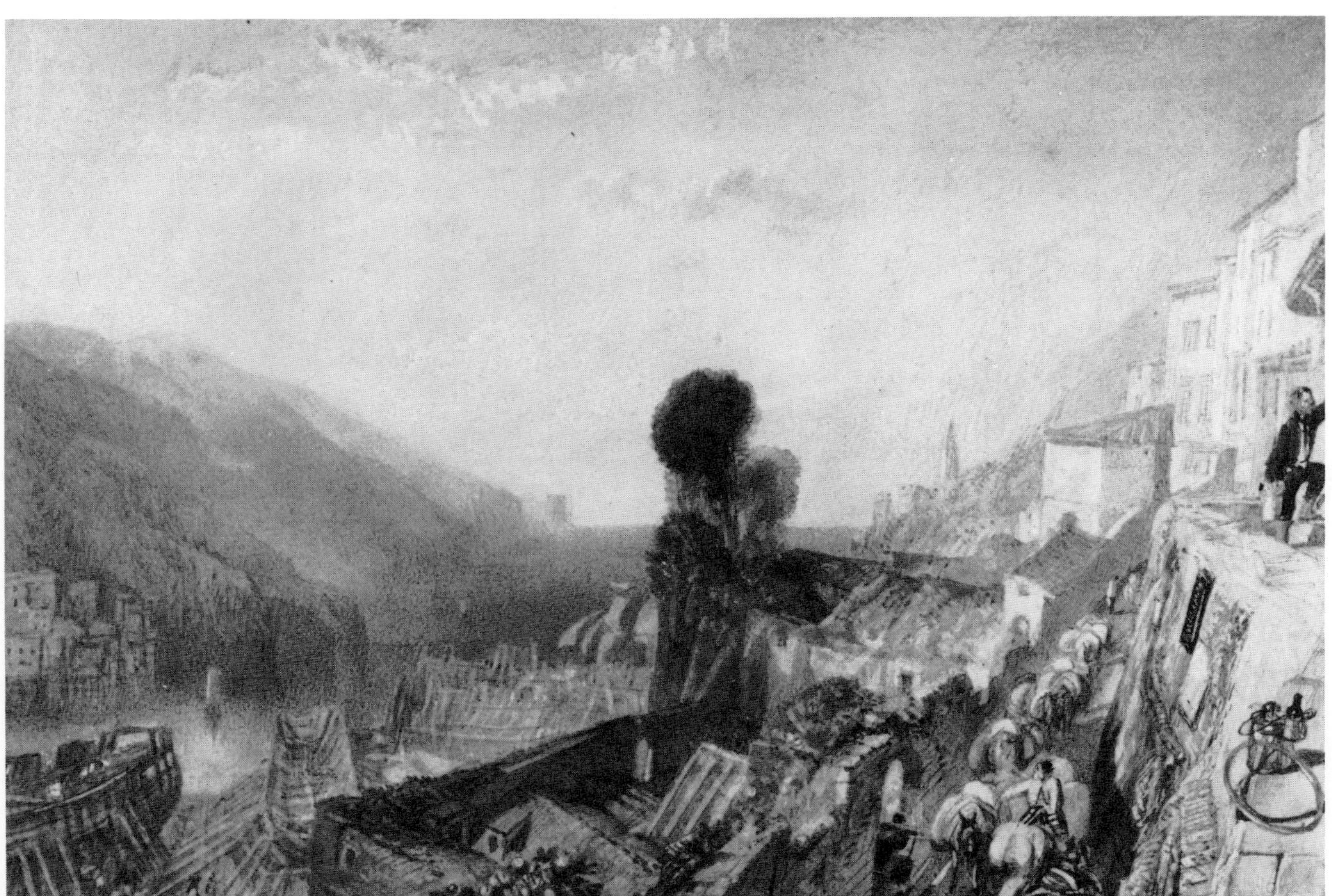

14 **Dartmouth on the River Dart** *c.* 1823

watercolor, $6\frac{3}{16} \times 8\frac{7}{8}$ in. (157 × 227 mm.)

TB CCVIII-C

This drawing was engraved by Samuel William Reynolds in 1825 as one of a series of mezzotints published between 1823 and 1827 under the title *The Rivers of England* (R.759). The project was planned by the engravers William Bernard and George Cooke with whom Turner had collaborated since 1811 in the production of the forty line engravings of *Picturesque Views of the Southern Coast of England*, parts of which began to appear in 1814 and continued to come out until 1826. The medium of mezzotint had received a fresh commercial stimulus from the development of the steel plate in about 1820, and Turner seems to have been particularly interested in working for mezzotinters since his own experiments on some of the later plates of the *Liber Studiorum* (see No. 8), which after about 1816 began to assume greater richness and darkness of tone, and were often actually engraved by Turner himself. This development was to lead to the "Little Liber Studiorum" set, made in the mid-1820s (see Nos. 17 and 20). The subject of the *Dartmouth* is a particularly splendid example of Turner's ample and expansive invention, and is conspicuous among the *Rivers* watercolors as being noticeably Italianate in flavor, whereas the majority share a very English atmosphere. The organization of the view round a steeply sloping perspective, dominated by a rather stylized tree and lit by a melting golden sky, reflects the plans of some of his oil paintings of imaginary historical or mythological Mediterranean subjects – *Dido Building Carthage*, for instance (1815; National Gallery, London)[1] or the sketch of *An Italian Hill Town*, of about 1828 (Tate Gallery).[2] But the circumstantial detail of lovingly observed local life is characteristic; despite the small scale of the drawing, and its grand design, he conveys a strong sense of real life: the shipbuilding yards indicate a central aspect of Dartmouth's economy, while the donkeys in the alley and the milkman making his rounds show his fascination with the activities of ordinary people, which he willingly elevates to the status of staffage in a heroic setting.

1 Repr. Herrmann, 1975, pl. 77.

2 Repr. Rothenstein and Butlin, 1964, pl. 75.

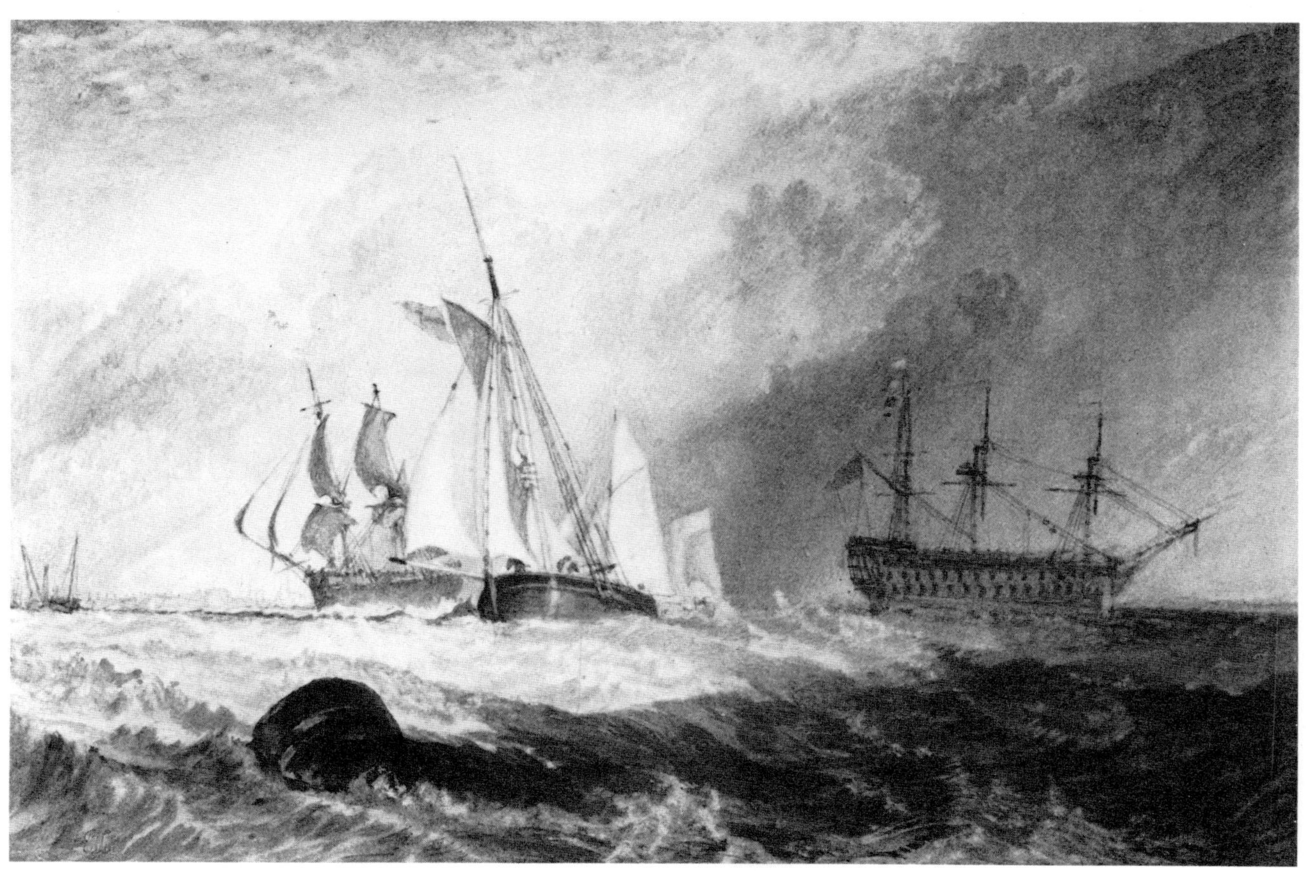

15 **Sheerness** *c.* 1825

watercolor, $6\frac{1}{4} \times 9\frac{7}{16}$ in. (159 × 239 mm.)

TB CCVIII-T

This design was engraved in mezzotint by Thomas Lupton in 1828 (R.783) as plate 5 of *The Ports of England*, a series conceived as a sequel to the *Rivers of England* (see No. 14) and issued between 1826 and 1828. Only six subjects were published, however, together with a wrapper design possibly etched by Turner, and the whole series of twelve plates did not appear until 1856, when it was published as *The Harbours of England* with a text by Ruskin. The *Ports* took Turner back to the kind of offshore marine subject that he was fond of in the first decade of the century, and this example returns, too, to his favorite scenes in the estuary of the Thames (compare, for instance, No. 8). A sketchbook of the early 1820s, the *Medway* book, TB CXCIX, contains many tiny pencil notes of the shoreline of Kent seen from a boat out on the water, and it is just such a glimpse of land that we get in the left background of this subject. Turner made several larger finished watercolors of similar scenes during these years (e.g. *Hastings, Deep-Sea Fishing*,[1] 1818, British Museum Lloyd Bequest, 1958-7-12-419, and *Dover Castle from the Sea*,[2] 1822, Boston Museum of Fine Arts). These are elaborate, fairly large-scale works; but the highly wrought drawings for the *Ports of England* offer, in miniature, the same degree of finish. Ruskin considered Sheerness "one of the noblest sea-pieces which Turner ever produced . . . the objects in it are few and noble, and the space infinite. The sky is quite one of his best: not violently black, but full of gloom and power . . . and the dim light entering along the horizon, full of rain, behind the ship of war, is true and grand in the highest degree" (*Harbours of England*, p. 37).

1 Repr. BM, 1975, No. 54, p. 46.

2 Repr. Berkeley, 1975, No. 19, p. 103.

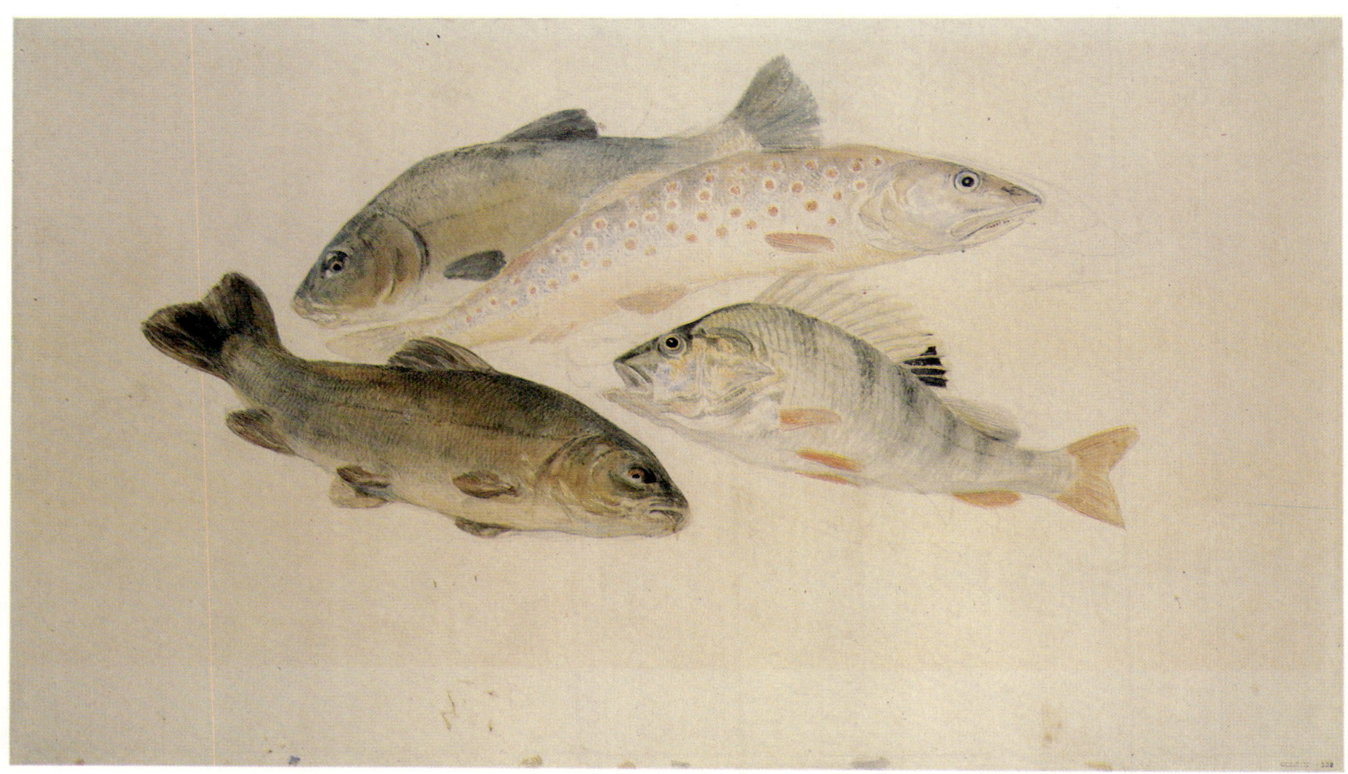

16 **Study of Four Fish** *c.* 1825–30

pencil and watercolor, $10\frac{3}{4} \times 18\frac{1}{2}$ in. (275 × 470 mm.)

TB CCLXIII-339

The meticulous technique with which Turner builds up elaborate subjects – on whatever scale – like those of Nos. 14 and 15, makes its appearance less frequently among the studies that he made as preparations for finished works. In this case, however, he lavished considerable care on rendering the textures of perch and trout, fish which he himself had perhaps just caught while staying with one of his patrons or friends; there are accounts of him fishing both in Yorkshire at Farnley, and in Sussex while staying with the Earl of Egremont at Petworth (see Nos. 22 to 25). Another study of perch similar to this is TB CCLXIII-338, and several other drawings of fish, probably made at a later date, also exist. It is difficult to place this sheet precisely, but the handling of the watercolor here has much in common with his treatment of finished drawings of the late 1820s. As early as 1807 he had shown himself a master of this type of still-life, when he painted the fish in the foreground of his *Sun Rising through Vapor*[1] (National Gallery, London) and probably about the time that he painted his *Slavers Throwing Overboard the Dead and Dying*[2] (1840; Museum of Fine Arts, Boston); he made further studies of fish, some in bodycolor; an example is the study of a *Gurnard* in the Victoria and Albert Museum, London.

1 Repr. Rothenstein and Butlin, 1964, pl. 28.

2 Repr. Herrmann, 1975, pl. 148.

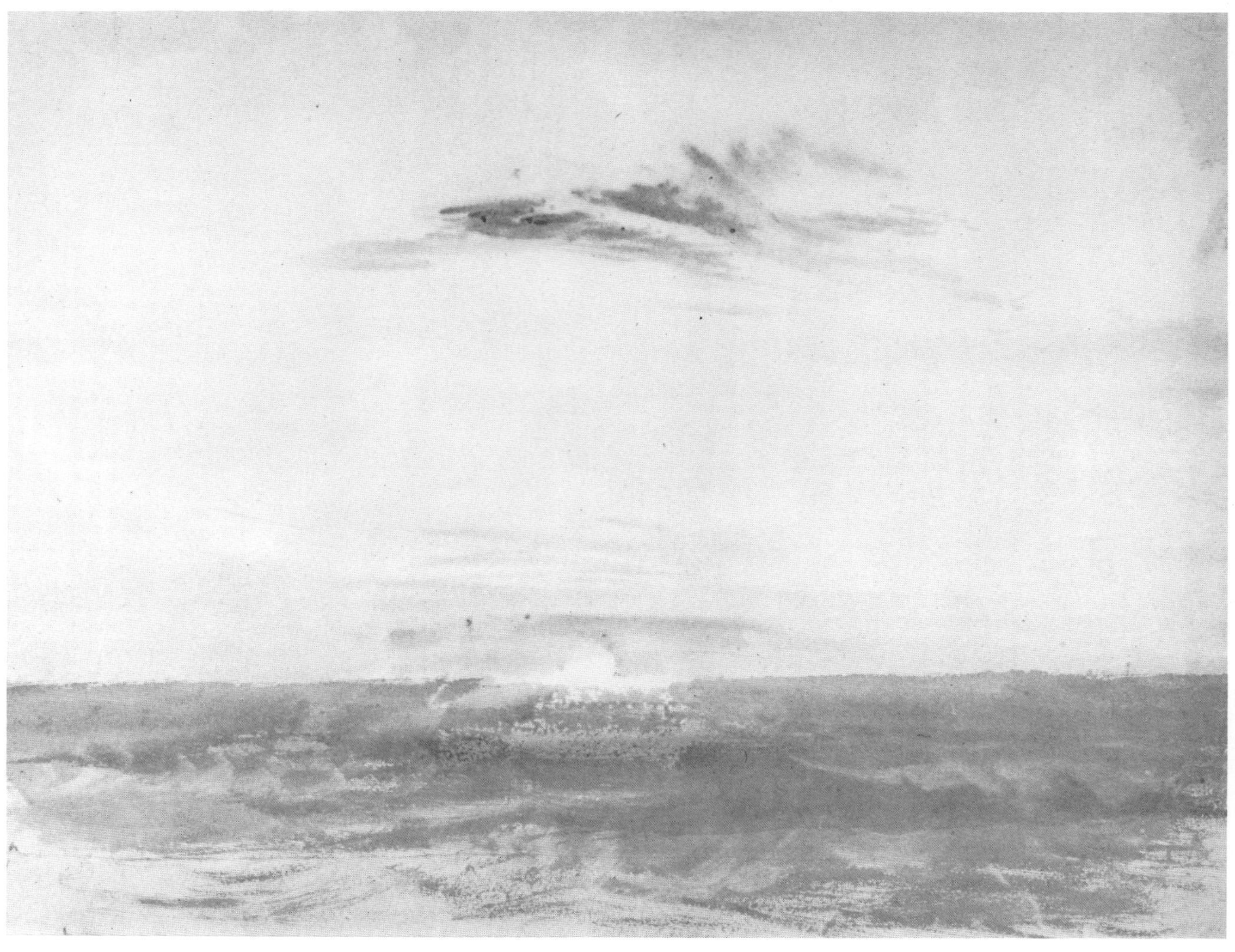

17 **Sunset Sky Over the Sea** *c.* 1825

watercolor, $11\frac{3}{4} \times 15\frac{3}{8}$ in. (298 × 392 mm.)

TB CCLXIII-68

This is apparently one of the group of sunset studies which are related to Turner's work on the dramatic sky effects in his mezzotint plates known as the "Little Liber Studiorum" (see note to No. 14 and also No. 20); but it is extremely difficult to say with any certainty when such drawings were made. A selection of them, with the suggestion that they could be grouped together and associated with the "Little Liber," is given in BM 1975, Nos. 97–103. Whether they were actually noted down from nature is almost impossible to ascertain; it is more likely that Turner made them as a sequence, within a very short space of time, either from his imagination or under the influence of some recent experience of a real sunset. It was always his typical method of working to produce series of studies (or even of finished works) which are closely related. In the case of many of these series, it may be that they were executed very rapidly at one sitting. Turner was exploring in these sky studies the potentialities of his art as much as the actual variety of the natural world.

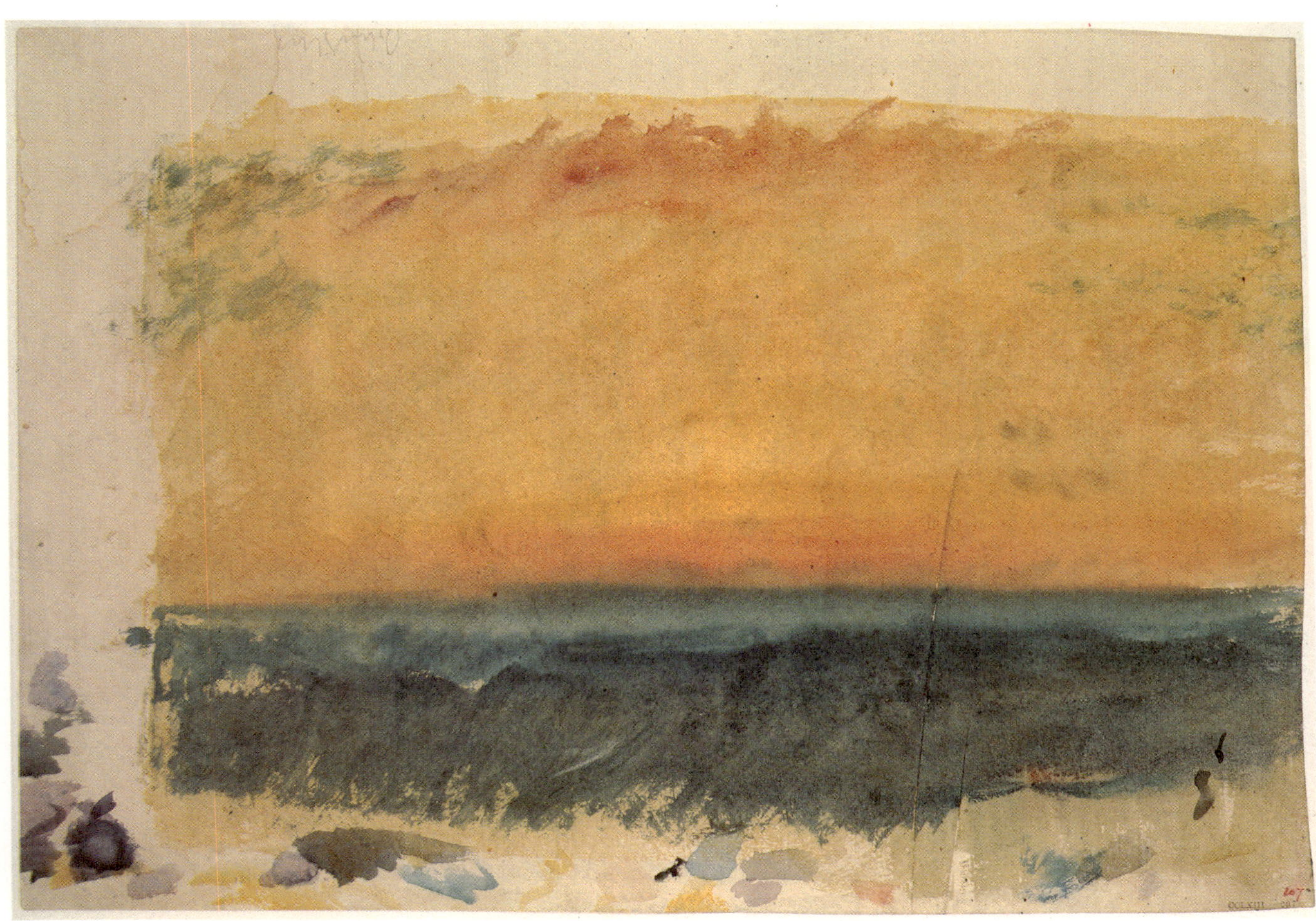

18 **Sunset Over the Sea (Crimson, Yellow, Blue, Green)** *c.* 1825

watercolor, $9\frac{3}{4} \times 13\frac{3}{4}$ in. (247 × 350 mm.)

TB CCLXIII-207

This is another study which may belong to the sequence of sunsets made in about 1825 (see No. 17). It is inscribed illegibly in the upper left corner; this may refer to a subject subsequently cut from the sheet. Turner often made several color studies on a single large sheet of paper and later separated them; he is also known to have done the same thing with oil on canvas (see RA 1974–5, Nos. 475–80).

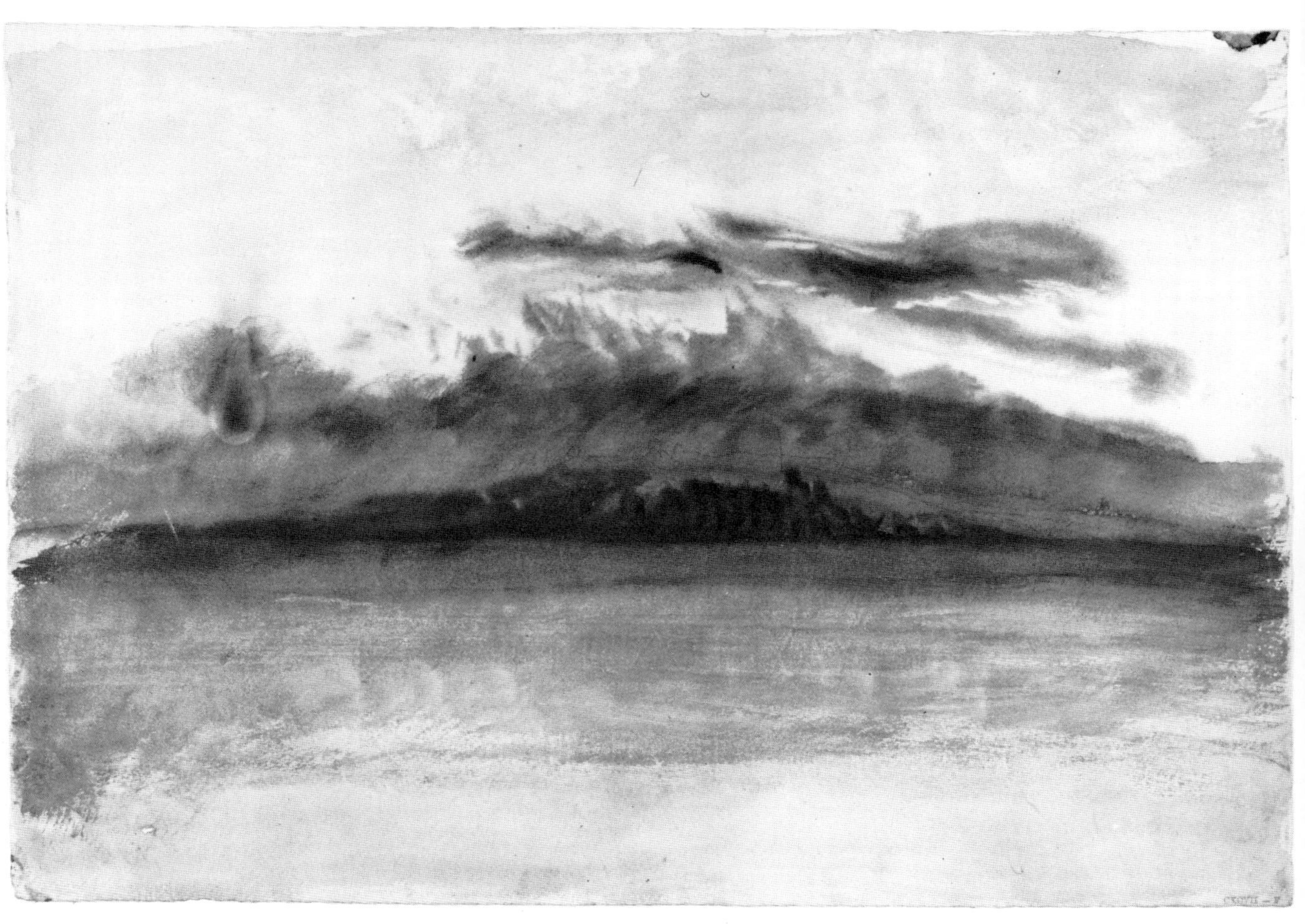

19 **Storm Clouds at Sunset** ?*c.* 1825

watercolor over pencil, $9\frac{1}{2} \times 13\frac{1}{2}$ in. (242 × 344 mm.)

TB CXCVII-F

This study, which is on a sheet of Whatman paper watermarked 1814, belongs to the large group of such drawings in the Turner Bequest which has yet to be satisfactorily arranged in terms of chronology. Finberg allocated the sheet to the years up to 1820; but in its rich use of pigment and in its preoccupation with the effects of a heavily clouded, dark-toned sky, it has much in common with the studies that Turner made in connection with his "Little Liber Studiorum," probably in the mid-1820s (see No. 20). He had experimented with pigment thickened with some such agent as flour paste at an early stage in his career (there is an example, TB LXX-O, which dates from about 1799), and the touching out of color with a dry brush that occurs in this sky study is also a device dating from that period; as he grew older such technical details disappeared from his color sketches, and he relied mainly on simple washes, sometimes strengthened with a pen; but in his finished watercolors processes like these remained a necessary feature of his technique.

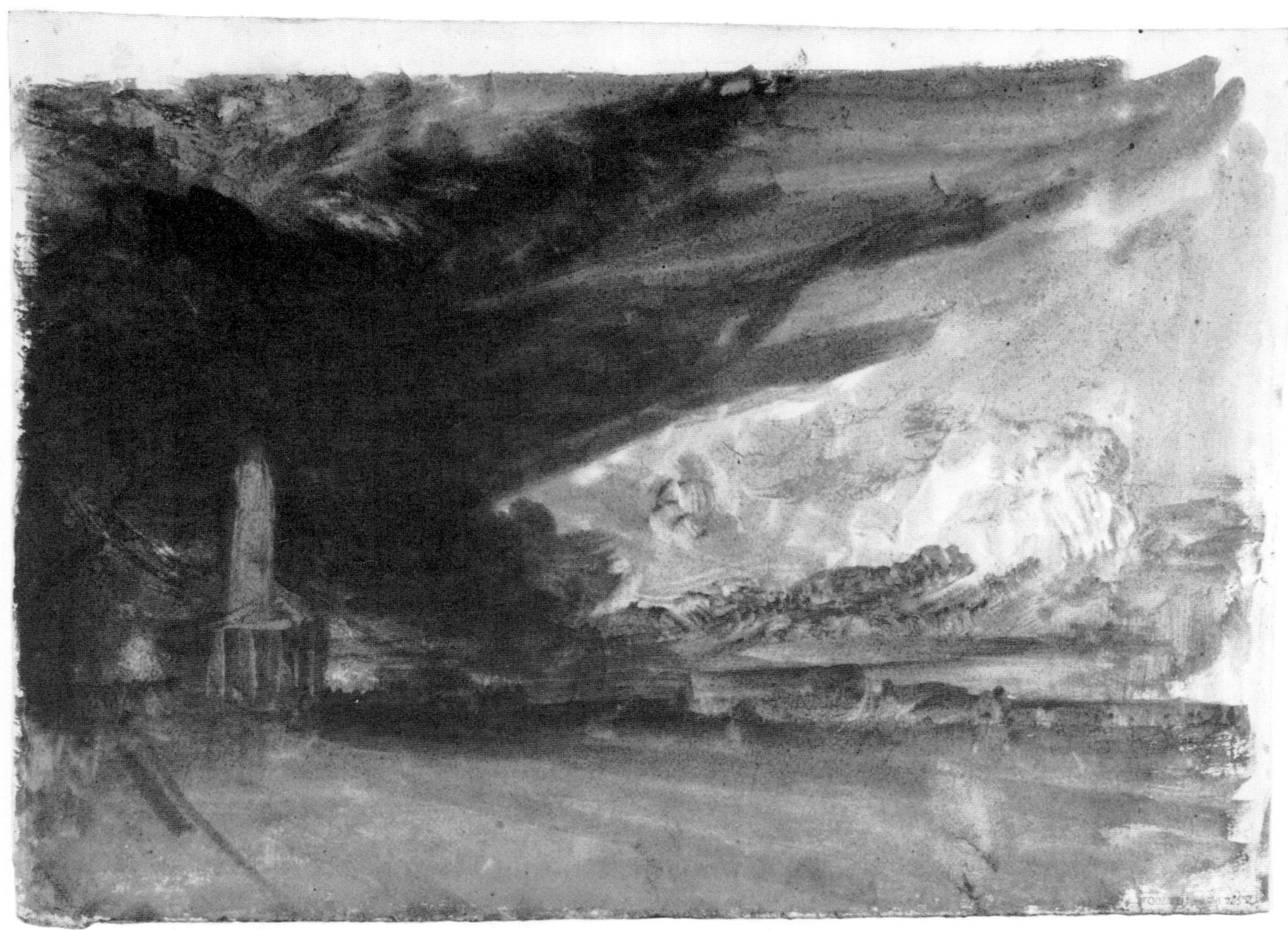

20 **A Stormy Landscape with an Obelisk and Classical Portico** *c.* 1825

watercolor, $8\frac{5}{8} \times 11\frac{3}{4}$ in. (219 × 298 mm.)

TB CCLXIII-252

There seems to be no possible identification for this strange landscape, in which heavy storm-clouds lower above what may be the ruins of a classical temple vaguely reminiscent of Paestum. It is very different in treatment and subject from a drawing which is certainly of *Paestum in a Thunderstorm*[1] (TB CCCLXIV-224), and which Turner used as the basis for one of the mezzotint plates in his so-called "Little Liber Studiorum" (R.799); but nevertheless this sheet may have some connection with that project, as Finberg suggested. The thick, rich application of color is typical of some of the studies Turner made at about the time of the "Little Liber" – i.e., presumably, *c.* 1825 – and the palette of inky blues recurs in a number of related sketches: for example, the *Harbor with Full Moon Behind Dark Clouds*[2] (TB CCLXIII-192) which was used for the "Little Liber" plate of *Shields Lighthouse*,[3] and which may also be connected with the *Shields on the River Tyne*[4] (TB CCVIII-V) mezzotinted for the *Rivers of England* series in 1823 (R.753). The generally accepted view that Turner was working on his "Little Liber" in about 1825 is perhaps corroborated by a mezzotint issued in 1826 by F. C. Lewis of a *Sunset at Sea After a Storm*[5] by Francis Danby (1793–1861); the picture had been shown at the Royal Academy in 1824. Lewis's print is very close in spirit to Turner's "Little Liber" plates, and it is quite possible that it provided the impulse for the series. The successful productions of his contemporaries often stimulated him to experiment in unfamiliar areas, and indeed were to have a formative effect on his art until the end of his career (see also No. 30).

1 Repr. RA, 1974–75, No. 252, p. 97.

2 Repr. BM, 1975, No. 89, p. 63.

3 Repr. Christopher White, *English Landscape, 1630–1850*, Yale Center for British Art, 1977, pls. CXVIII and CXXIX.

4 Repr. Walker, 1976, fig. 23, p. 23.

5 Repr. Eric Adams, *Francis Danby: Varieties of Poetic Landscape*, pl. 34.

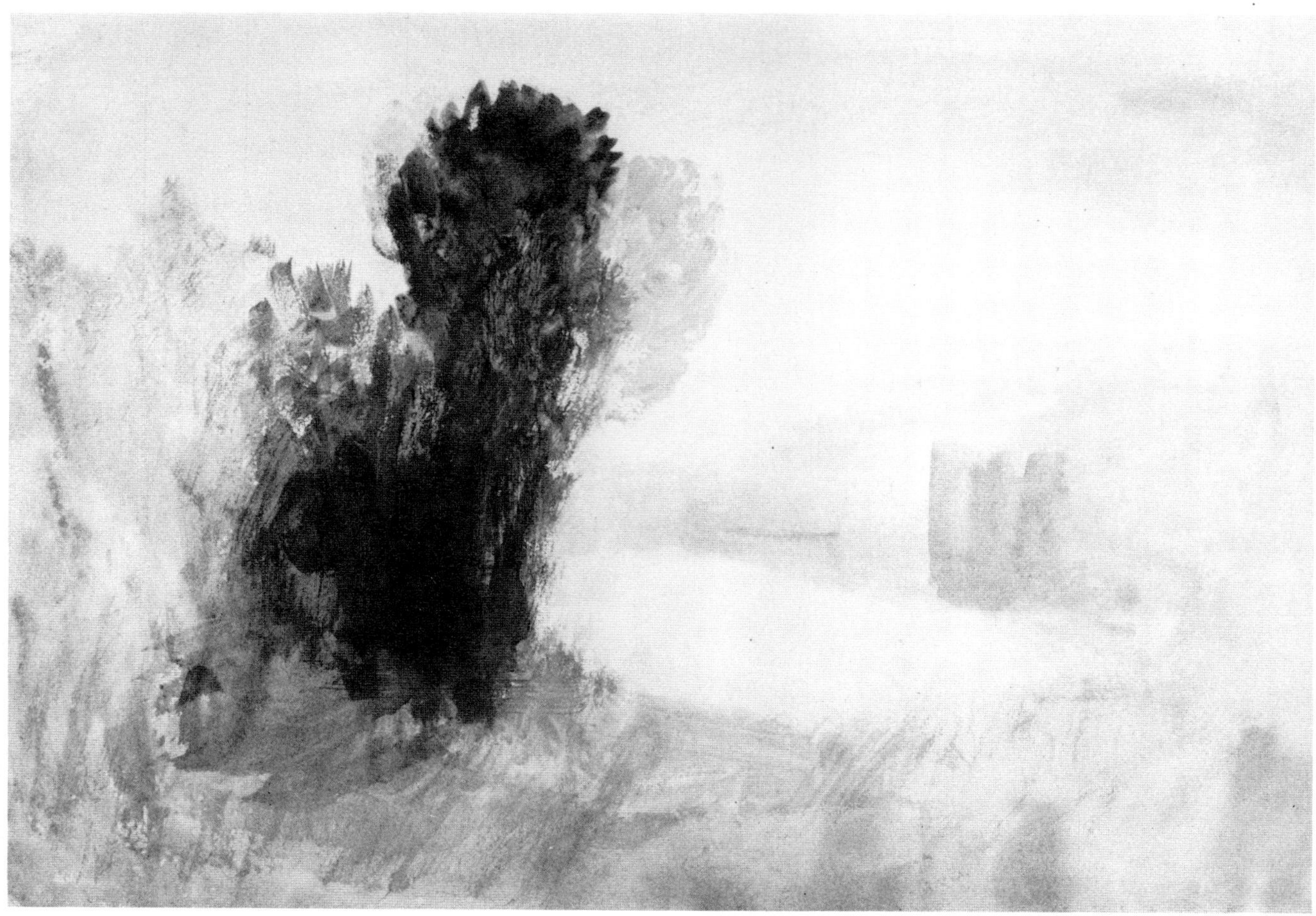

21 **Classical Landscape Composition** ?*c.* 1828

watercolor, $13\frac{3}{16} \times 18\frac{15}{16}$ in. (336 × 480 mm.)

TB CCLXIII-180

There are a number of studies of this type in the Turner Bequest (e.g. TB CCLXIII-65, 189; a few exist in other collections); they may be connected with the artist's activities in Rome in 1828, and some have been associated with *Ulysses Deriding Polyphemus*[1] of that year (National Gallery, London) but they are equally relevant to paintings with classical compositions of both earlier and later dates. The handling of watercolor here is not unlike that of the "Little Liber" series (see No. 17) but the paler color-range and open, airy plan are reminiscent of the color-beginnings for *England and Wales* subjects of about 1830–35. It is possible, indeed, that this is a preliminary color scheme for one of the drawings in that set: Turner often imposed classicizing, Italianate plans on English views (compare *Dartmouth*, No. 14) and there are some examples of that procedure among the *England and Wales* watercolors (notably *Prudhoe Castle*[2] of about 1827; British Museum, Lloyd Bequest, 1958-7-12-428).

1 Repr. Herrmann, 1975, pls. 106 and 107.

2 Repr. BM, 1975, No. 106, p. 70.

22 **In Petworth Park** *c.* 1828

bodycolor on blue paper, $5\frac{1}{2} \times 7\frac{1}{2}$ in. (140 × 191 mm.)

TB CCXLIV-10

A very indistinct impression using ocher, pink and mauve, this view is difficult to identify precisely. It may show the same subject as No. 24, which is itself hard to place. Turner's use of small pieces torn from a larger folded sheet of blue paper is common to the Petworth series and to the drawings made in connection with the project for illustrations of the *Great Rivers of Europe*, advertized in 1833 by Charles Heath, the publisher of the *Picturesque Views in England and Wales*. See Nos. 25 and 34.

23 **In Petworth Park: Looking Towards the Lake** *c.* 1828

watercolor and bodycolor on blue paper, $5\frac{3}{8} \times 7\frac{7}{16}$ in. (137 × 188 mm.)

TB CCXLIV-11

Unlike the other two subjects on this mat (Nos. 22 and 24), this view can be confidently identified as a scene in the park at Petworth, looking across the lawn towards the lake. It is therefore probable that Turner executed it along with the series of interiors at Petworth (see Nos. 25 to 33) which may have been made in a short space of time during a single visit to the house.

24 **In Petworth Park: Looking Across the Lake** *c.* 1828

watercolor and bodycolor on blue paper, $5\frac{3}{8} \times 7\frac{3}{8}$ in. (139 × 188 mm.)

TB CCXLIV-12

This view is known as "Petworth," but it is hardly distinguishable in style and mood from drawings like TB CCLIX-70, which is called a view on the Seine, and has been thought to show St. Germain-en-Laye. Apart from the fact that they are all on small sheets of blue paper, there are strong similarities, stylistic and otherwise, between the Petworth and "Rivers of Europe" drawings (see No. 34) and it may be that Turner worked on the French designs while staying at Petworth after a tour of the Seine in 1829, though it has been suggested that the Petworth drawings were done a year or two earlier (see No. 25). Another drawing over which confusion has arisen is TB CCLIX-5, which Finberg called *A French Château*, but which is evidently a view of Petworth house from the lake.

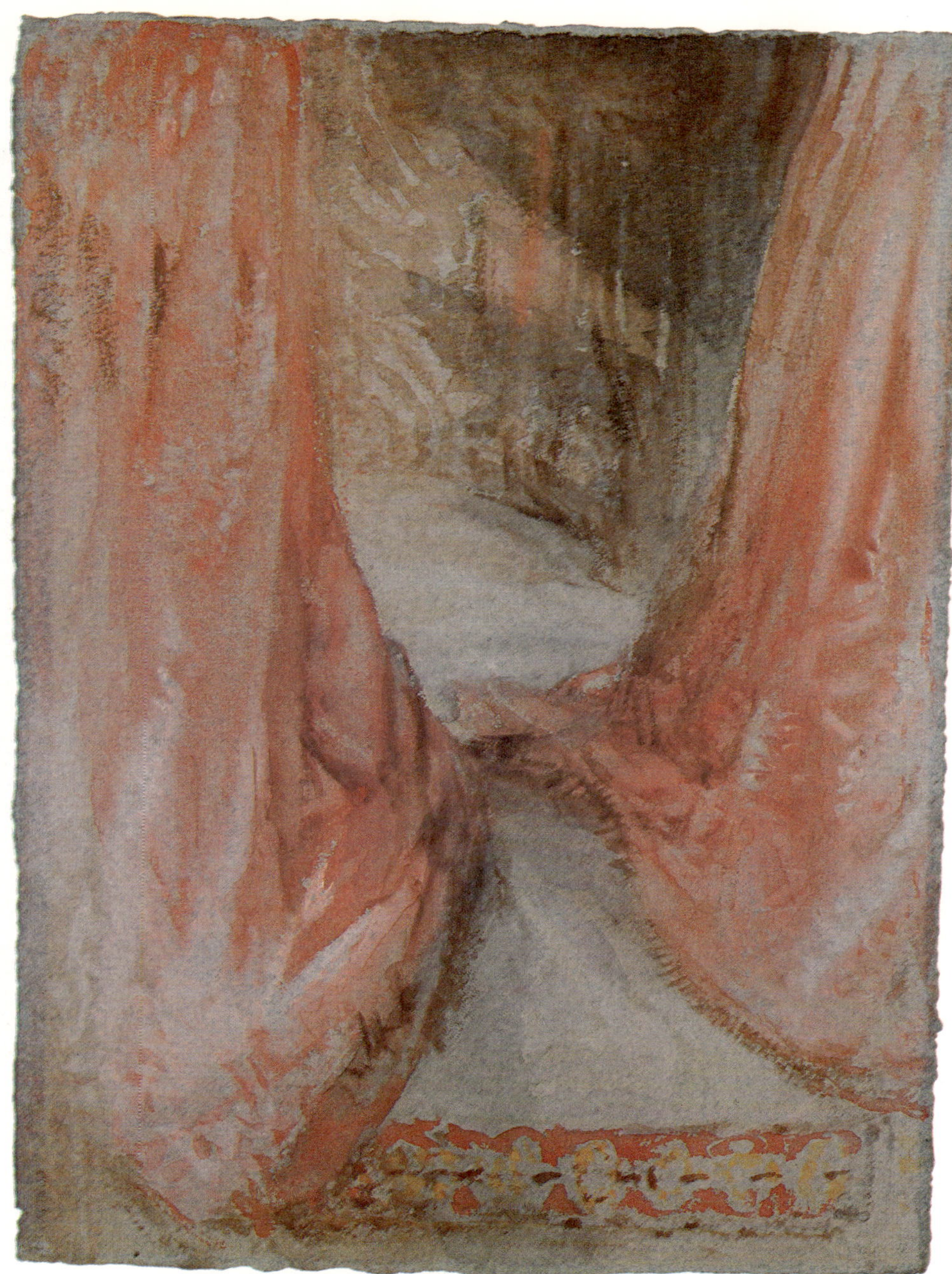

Petworth: Study of a Bed with Pink Satin Curtains
c. 1828

watercolor and bodycolor on blue paper, $7\frac{11}{16} \times 5\frac{1}{2}$ in. (194 × 140 mm.)

TB CCXLIV-15

Turner is now known to have visited Lord Egremont at Petworth in August of 1827, immediately after a stay at East Cowes Castle with the architect John Nash. It was there that he made studies of Cowes regatta and the castle for two views executed for Nash and exhibited in 1828; one, *East Cowes Castle: the Regatta Beating to Windward*,[1] is now in the Indianapolis Museum of Art. Turner also made a number of little studies on blue paper, with a pen and some chinese white, showing details of the castle and groups of figures in conversation. These, although in a different medium, are very similar in mood to the famous Petworth drawings, of which this is an example. In fact, Turner did use a pen in some of his Petworth studies: the hitherto misidentified view TB CCLIX-5, mentioned in the entry to No. 24, is colored, but has a full outline in pen and ink. The similarity of these drawings to those made by Turner for the "Rivers of Europe" project, which were in hand probably over a number of years between 1826 and 1834, makes any exact dating impossible. Turner continued to stay on occasion at Petworth until Lord Egremont's death in 1837. Turner had made watercolors of domestic subjects before, notably for Walter Fawkes in the set of views of Farnley Hall that he drew in about 1818, but the Petworth group strikes a new note of intimacy and intensity; it is possible that by this time Turner had become aware of the lush little historical interiors of R. P. Bonington (1802–29) which were acquired by London dealers from about 1827, and set himself to imitate some of their quality.

1 Repr. Herrmann, 1975, pl. 119.

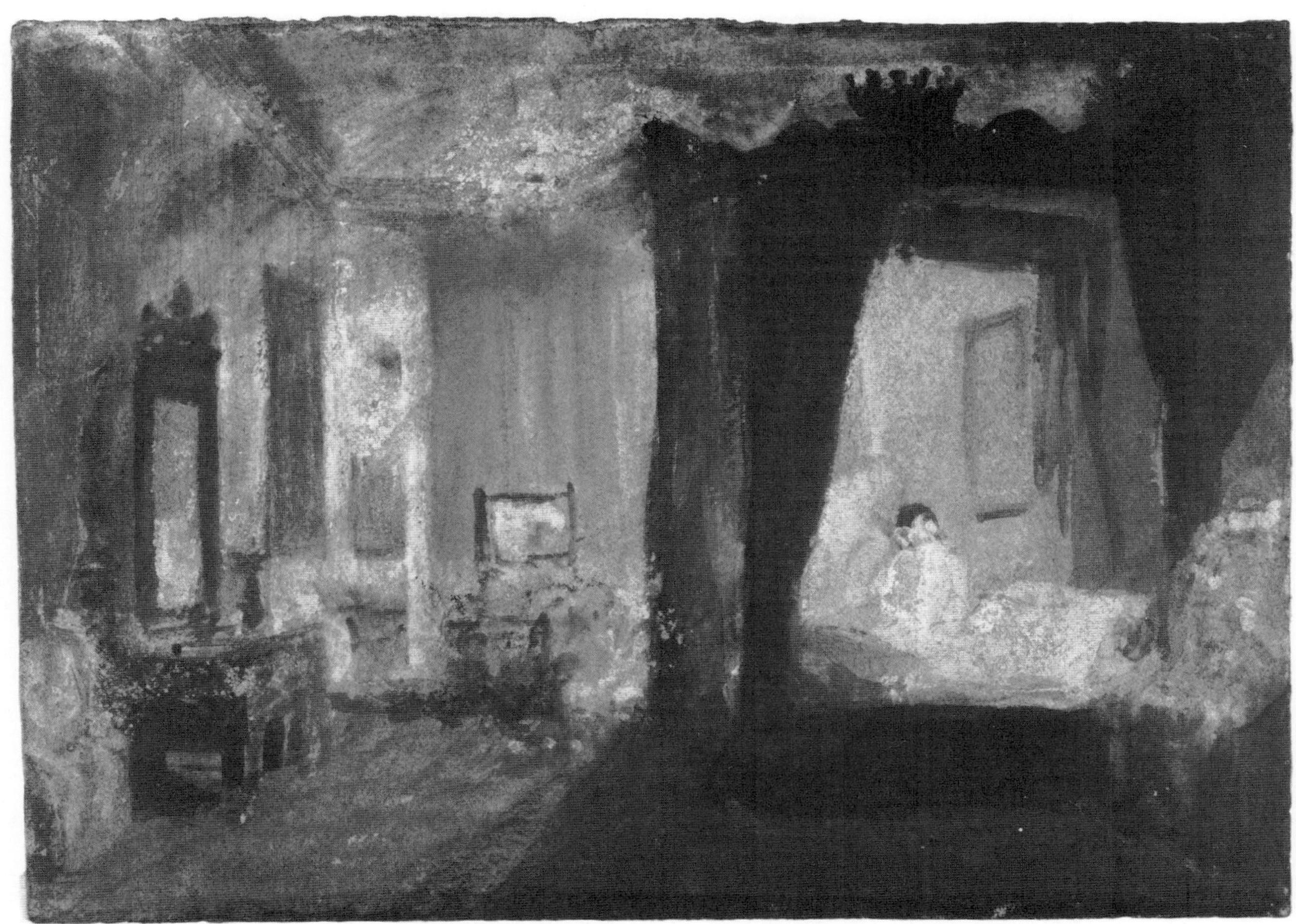

26 **Petworth: A Bedroom with a Large Four-Poster Bed** *c.* 1828

watercolor and bodycolor on blue paper, $5\frac{3}{8} \times 7\frac{1}{2}$ in. (138 × 189 mm.)

TB CCXLIV-17

The fact that Turner had access to so many of the bedrooms at Petworth has occasioned some surprise, and the suggestion of intimacy has led to an association of these drawings with the *Color Studies No. 1* sketchbook (TB CCXCI [b]) in which a number of erotic scenes in bedrooms occur. There need not, in fact, be any connection; but there is no reason why Turner should not have been given permission to wander fairly freely round the house with a sheaf of his torn sheets of blue paper in hand. We know that Leslie (see No. 30) also made studies of this kind at Petworth.

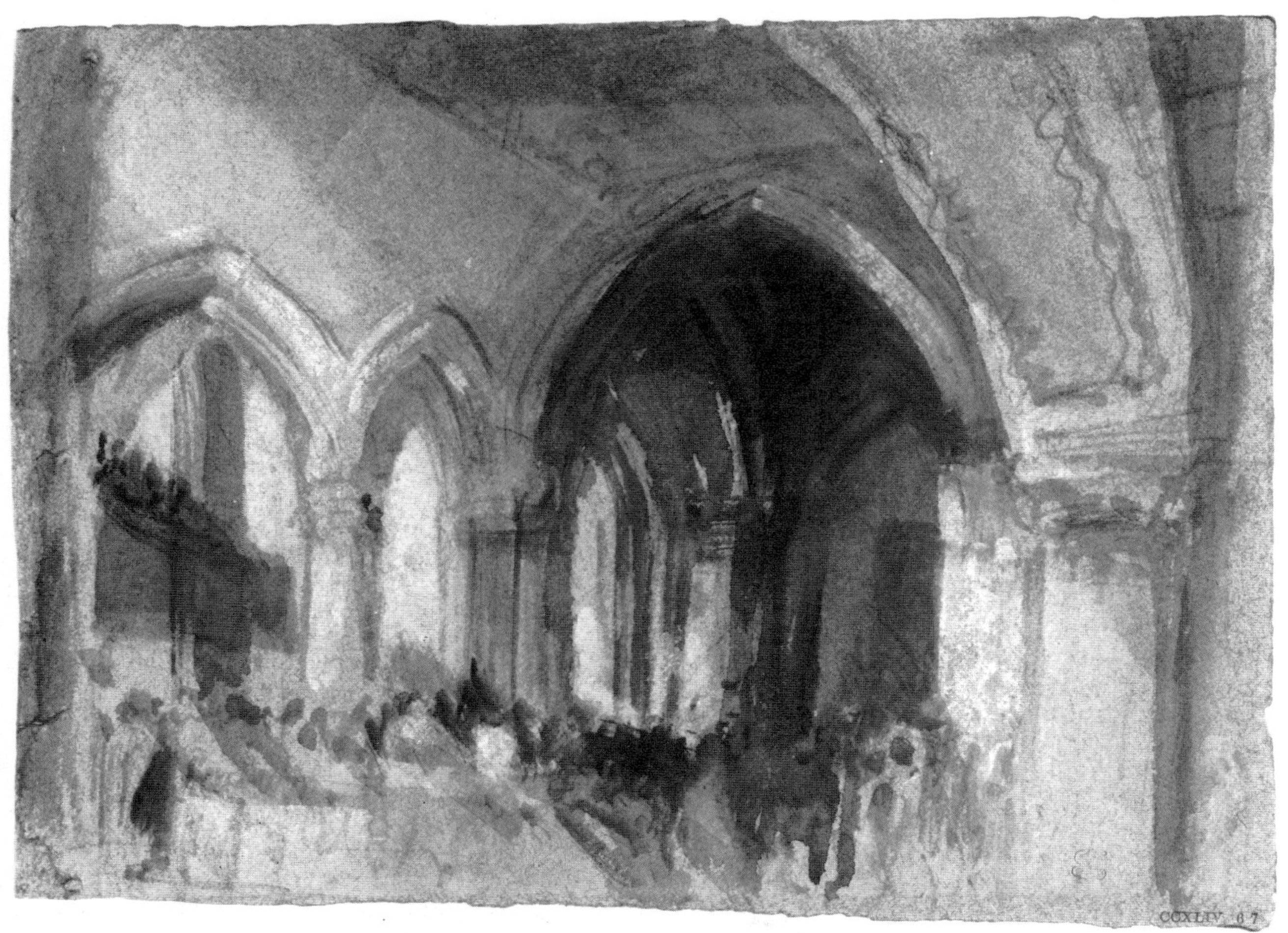

27 **Petworth: Interior of the Church** *c.* 1828

watercolor and bodycolor over pencil on blue paper, $5\frac{9}{16} \times 7\frac{7}{16}$ in. (141 × 189 mm.)

TB CCXLIV-67

This study is unusual among the Petworth drawings in having pencil-work under the color. We might infer from this that Turner did not work direct with the colors from the subject here; and indeed it is a little unlikely (though not impossible) that he would have taken such equipment with him to church. Perhaps the whole sequence of scenes during a church service at Petworth (see also No. 28) were done from memory. We have no evidence, for that matter, that any of the other Petworth studies were done from life; but the church interiors are not executed in the wide range of colors common to most of the other drawings, and this may be an indication that Turner did work on the spot, with limited materials, while the other scenes were noted directly on the spot with a full gamut of color.

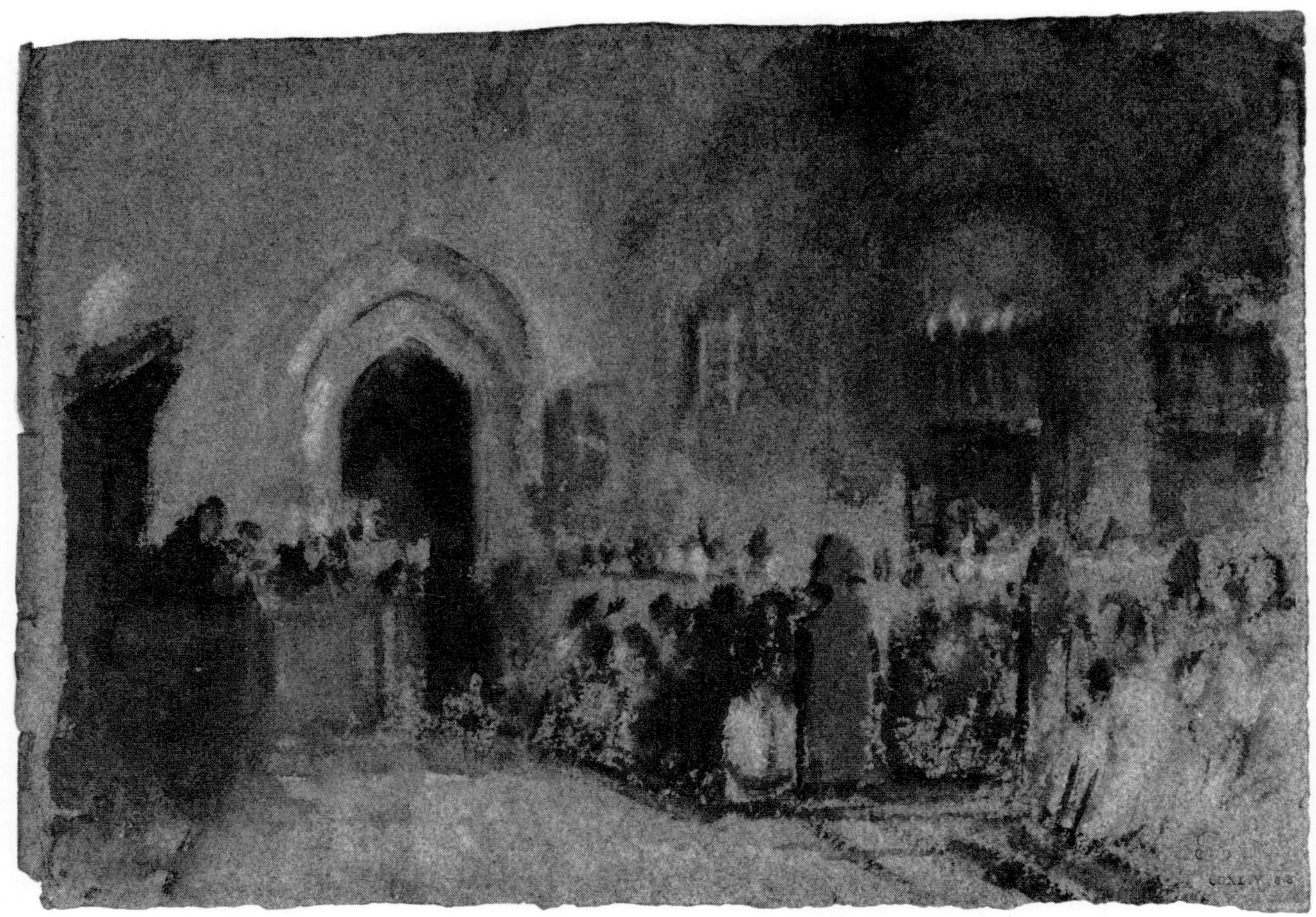

28 **Petworth: Interior of the Church** *c.* 1828

watercolor and bodycolor on blue paper, $5\frac{1}{2} \times 7\frac{1}{2}$ in. (140 × 192 mm.)

TB CCXLIV-68

See No. 27 for comments on the series of drawings that Turner made in the church at Petworth.

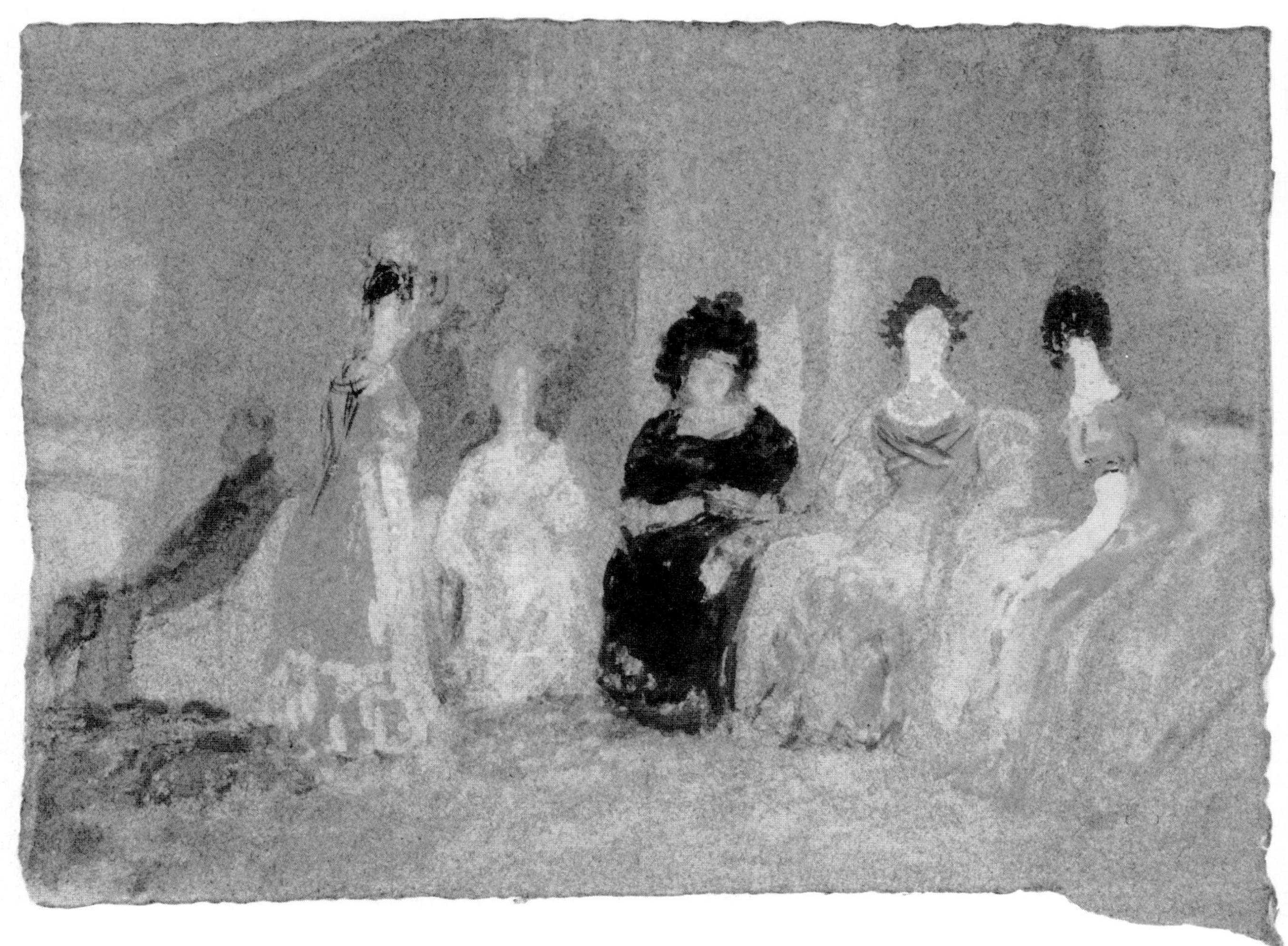

29 **Petworth: a Group of Ladies Conversing** *c.* 1828

bodycolor on blue paper, $5\frac{1}{2} \times 7\frac{1}{2}$ in. (140 × 191 mm.)

TB CCXLIV-101

This drawing is characteristic of the intimate atmosphere of the Petworth series, beautifully conveying the particularity of a domestic scene without elaborating detail, and making use of a rich effect of lighting that reflects Turner's revived interest in the work of Rembrandt at this period, an interest particularly noticeable in the paintings of Petworth House itself. There is also a suggestion of the influence of Bonington (see No. 25).

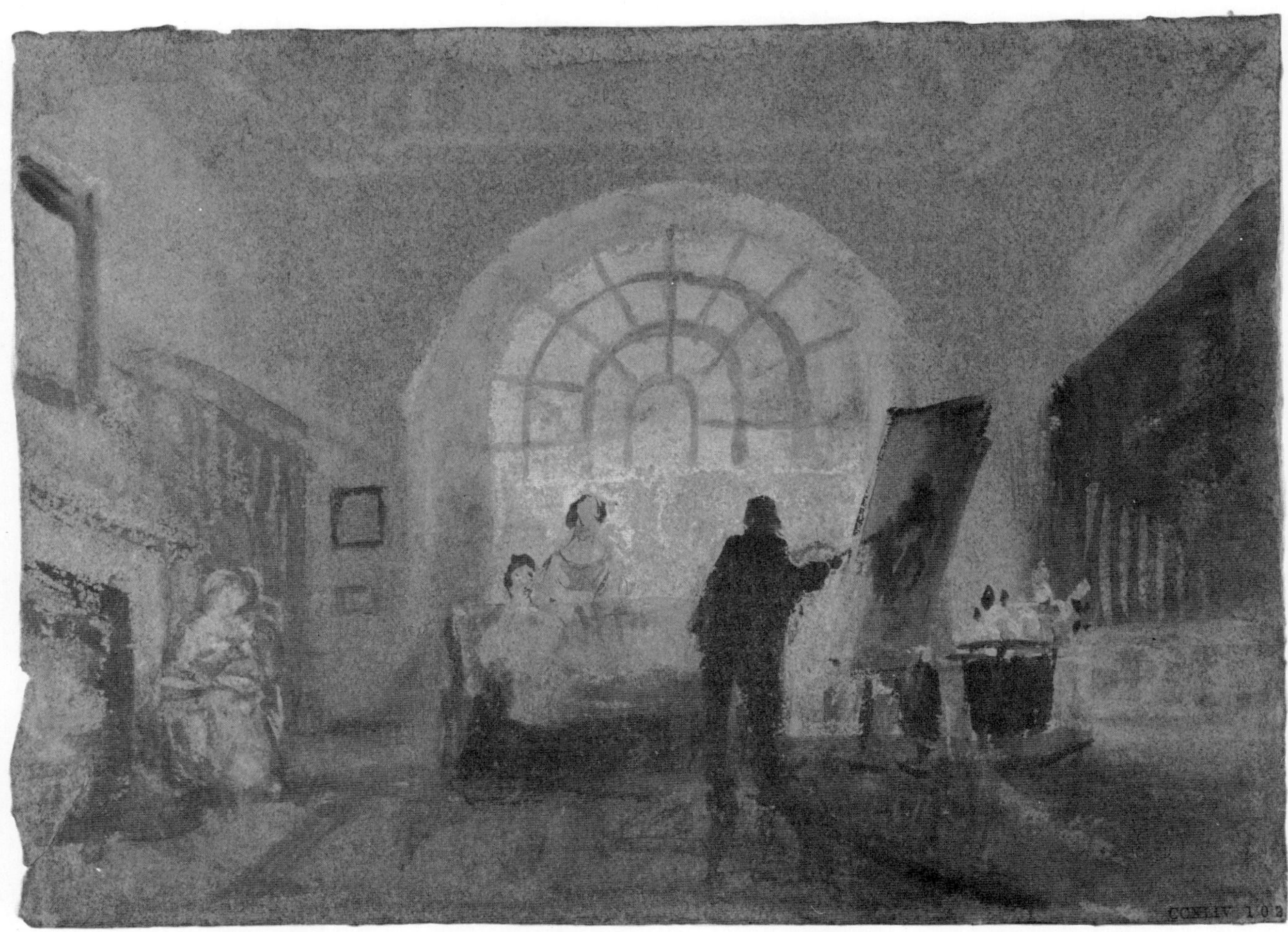

30 **Petworth: An Artist Painting in a Room with a Large Fanlight** *c.* 1828

bodycolor on blue paper, $5\frac{1}{2} \times 7\frac{1}{2}$ in. (140 × 189 mm.)

TB CCXLIV-102

Turner was one of several artists whom Lord Egremont both patronized and entertained; among them were Turner's friend (later one of his executors) George Jones, R.A. (1786–1869), Henry Thomson (1773–1843), and the American C. R. Leslie (1799–1859), Constable's biographer. Turner was allocated a studio of his own and so probably were these other painters; it is not clear which of them appears in this drawing, though we may imagine that Turner has represented himself, engaged in painting the portraits of the ladies, as in *The Letter*,[1] (Tate Gallery 5501) or even, perhaps, a more fanciful figure subject such as the *Music Party*,[2] (Tate Gallery 3550). Just as Egremont's collection of Old Masters contributed to a renewal of Turner's interest in several of them, so the living artists he met at Petworth seem to have stimulated him to feats of emulation; the young C. R. Leslie, in particular, was apparently a spur to his producing a number of paintings of historical figure subjects around 1830.

1 Repr. Jean Selz, *Turner*, 1975, p. 49.

2 Repr. RA, 1974–75, No. 336, p. 72.

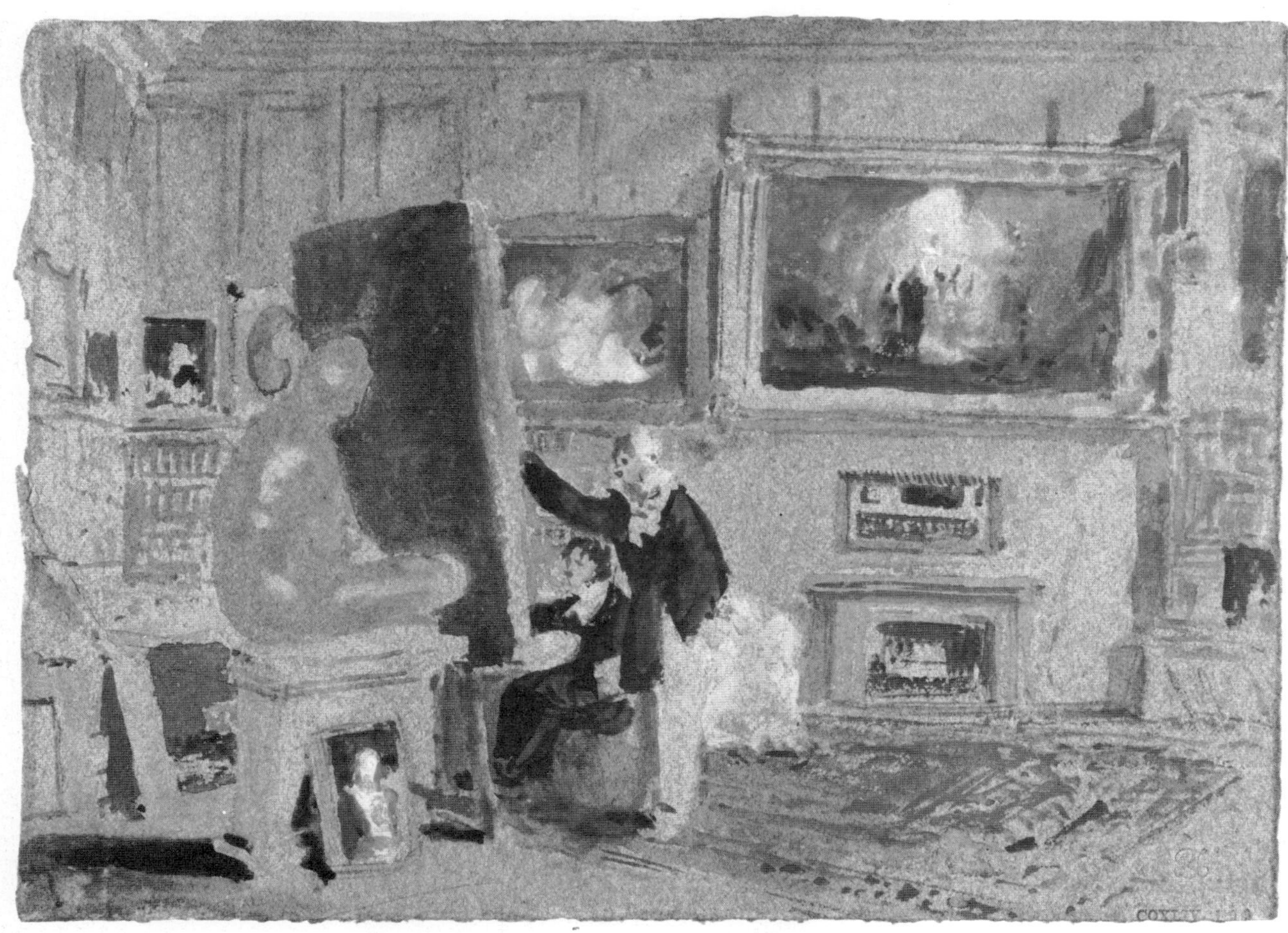

31 Petworth: Two Artists Painting *c.* 1828

bodycolor on blue paper, $5\frac{1}{2} \times 7\frac{3}{8}$ in. (139 × 188 mm.)

TB CCXLIV-103

This sheet provides further evidence of the activity of Lord Egremont's artist guests (see No. 30), and of his existing collection of works of art – paintings, sculptures, miniatures, and cameos. The mood here is very much that of the traditional "academy" interior, a *genre* that had been popular since the Renaissance in the representation of great collections and their owners, and practised by artists such as Zoffany and Turner's contemporary John Scarlett Davis (1804–44). In this case, we receive the impression that the two artists are engaged in copying some picture on the wall to the left. The large picture on the wall behind them bears a resemblance to Turner's own enigmatic canvas *Interior at Petworth*[1] (Tate Gallery 1988) but is unlikely to have any connection with that work, which is now thought to have been executed in memory of Lord Egremont after his death in 1837 (see R.A. 1974–75, No. 339).

1 Repr. Walker, 1976, pl. 32, p. 127.

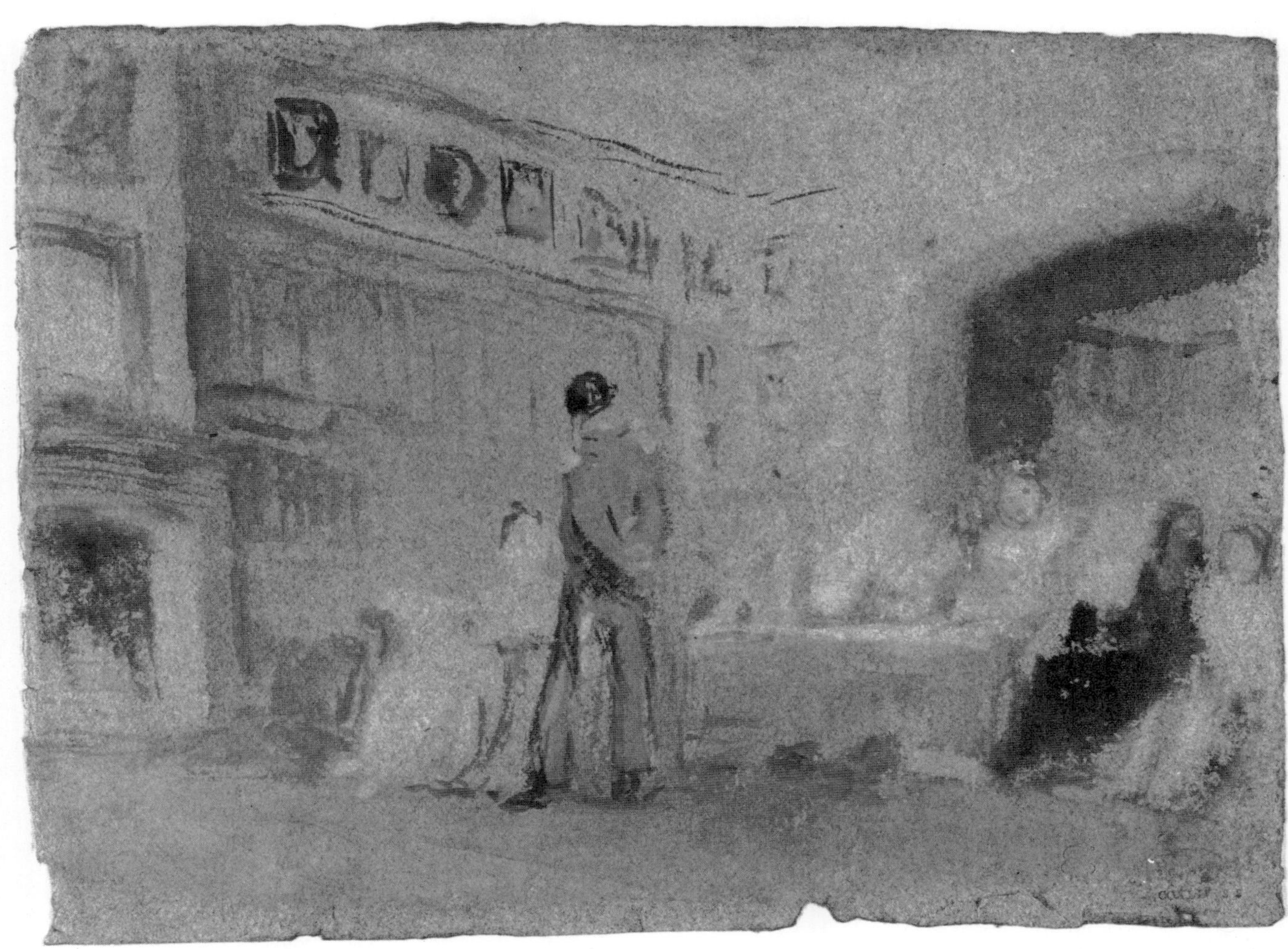

32 **Petworth: An Officer in Red Uniform Talking to a Seated Woman** *c.* 1828

bodycolor on blue paper, $5\frac{9}{16} \times 7\frac{1}{2}$in. (142 × 190 mm.)

TB CCXLIV-22

Like many of the Petworth drawings, this is a vivid representation of an informal moment rapidly noted on the spot, though it is quite possible that it was made from memory after Turner had observed it. The scene is the Library, though there is no attempt in this study to record the red color of the walls, a salient feature of the room (see No. 33).

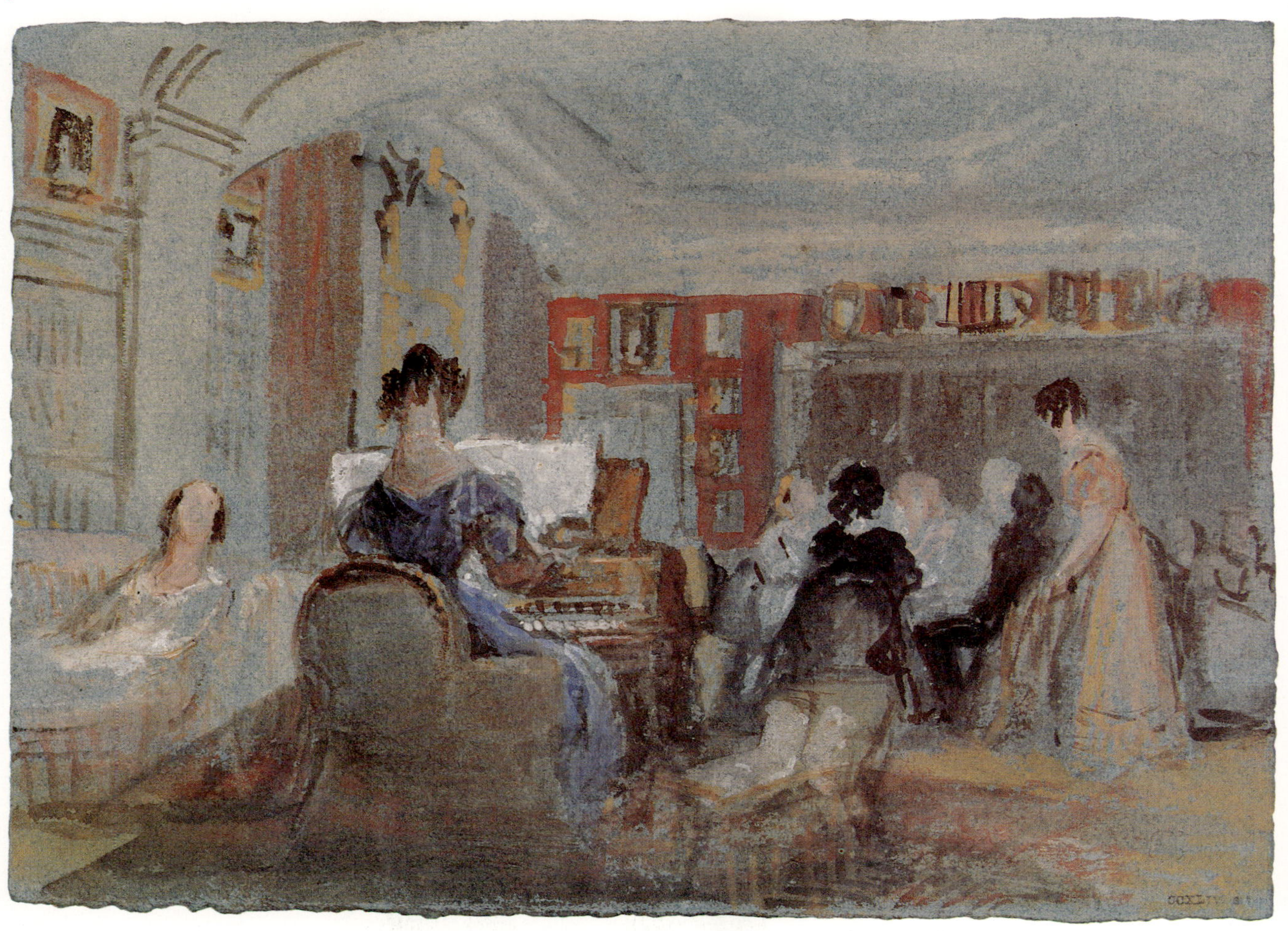

33 **Petworth: A Lady Playing the Spinet in the Library** *c.* 1828

bodycolor on blue paper, $5\frac{1}{2} \times 7\frac{1}{2}$ in. (140 × 190 mm.)

TB CCXLIV-37

Turner made a general view of the Library, with the spinet, in another drawing, TB CCXLIV-16, which is a masterly evocation of the spirit of a beautiful room without figures – a style of subject that he had already practised at Farnley in about 1818. Here he records an evening recital which may have provided the "raw material" for the fantasy *Music Party, Petworth* (Tate Gallery 3550), cast in a more sombre key and reflecting the combined influences of Rembrandt and Watteau. Other Petworth drawings, TB CCXLIV-28, 43, also record musical evenings: Turner's own interest in music has been demonstrated by Jack Lindsay (*J. M. W. Turner, His Life and Work*, p. 39); he is known to have played the flute, though there is no evidence that he performed for the benefit of Lord Egremont's guests.

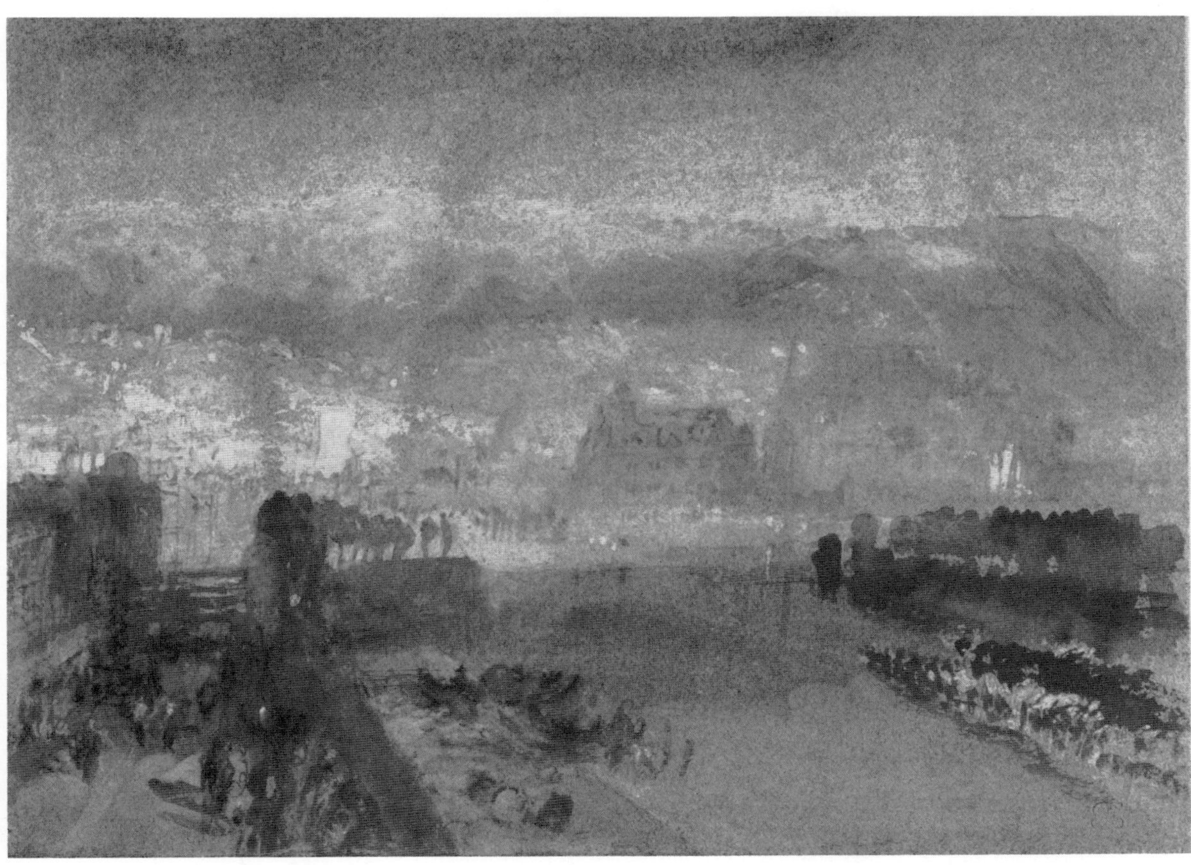

34 A Town on the Bènd of a River ?*c.* 1826

bodycolor on blue paper with some pen and red color,
$5\frac{9}{16} \times 7\frac{1}{2}$ in. (141 × 190 mm.)
TB CCLIX-99

When Turner first began work on Charles Heath's proposed "Great Rivers of Europe," in about 1826, he may have considered that notes made on the Seine in 1821 provided sufficient information about that river for his purposes, though he did in fact revisit it in 1829 (see No. 38); but he set off almost immediately to collect material on the Loire, the Meuse and the Moselle, in the summer of 1826. The drawings that he produced as a result of these journeys were evidently made with a view to finished work for the engraver, but only the *Loire* and *Seine* series were published (see Nos. 38 and 40) and much of the remaining mass of work is extemely difficult to identify. This drawing appears to represent the city of Liège, on the Meuse, seen from a point upstream; another view, looking downstream, is perhaps TB CCLIX-178. The coloring of the design, with its dominant oranges and greens, is that of many of the *Meuse* drawings, and differs from the warmer purples and reds of the *Loire* set, or the sunny ochers and blues of the *Seine*. The sheet appears to be in a state that is more or less "finished," that is to say, much as Turner would have sent it to the engraver; as the *Meuse* tour was never published, however, no print exists of the subject, and the identification of the view is conjectural.

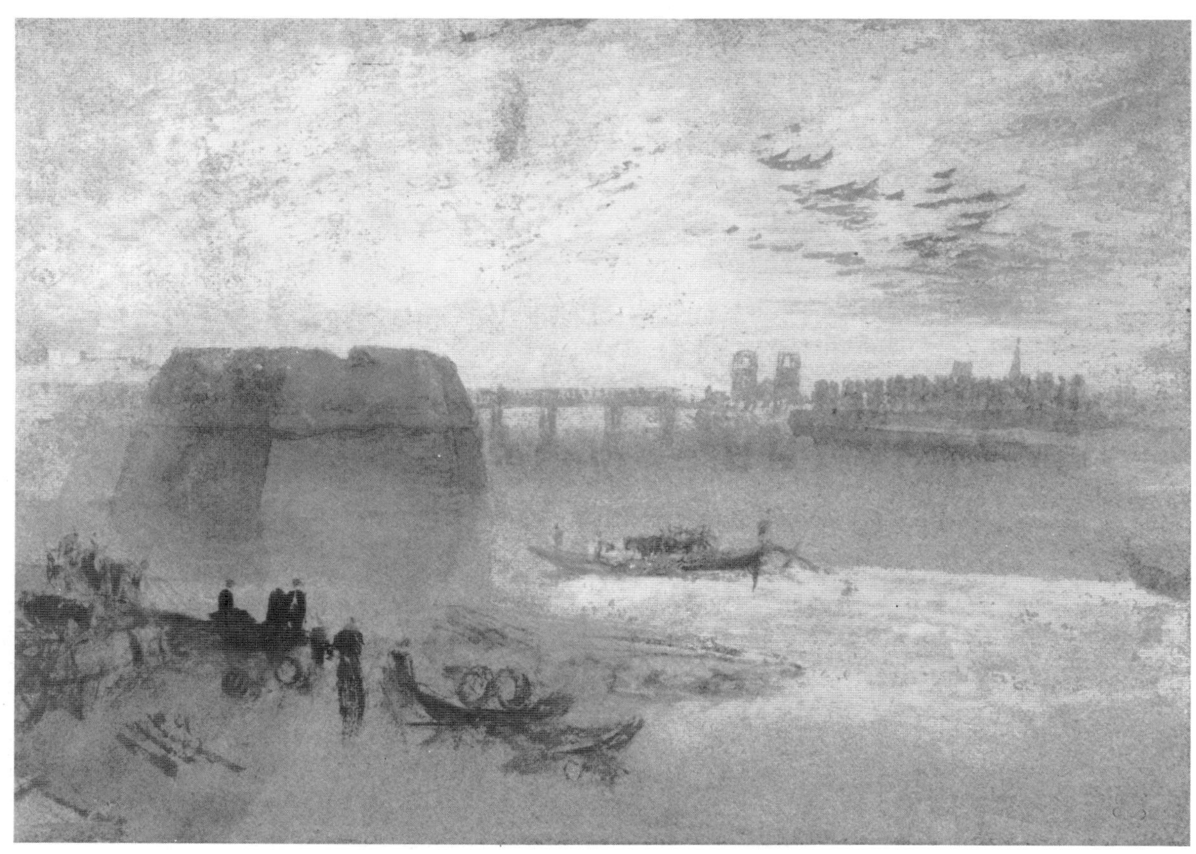

35 **A Town on a River with a Fort, and Distant Twin Towers** *c.* 1830

watercolor and bodycolor on blue paper, $5\frac{7}{16} \times 7\frac{1}{2}$in. (138 × 190 mm.)

ṪB CCLIX-100

As in the case of No. 34, this drawing has not been precisely identified; but it seems likely that it is an unpublished design from the series that Turner made for his *Wanderings by the Seine*, issued as the second and third "Annual Tours" of 1834 and '35. It may be that the town shown is Troyes, of which a different view was engraved by C. Armytage for the 1835 volume (R.492).

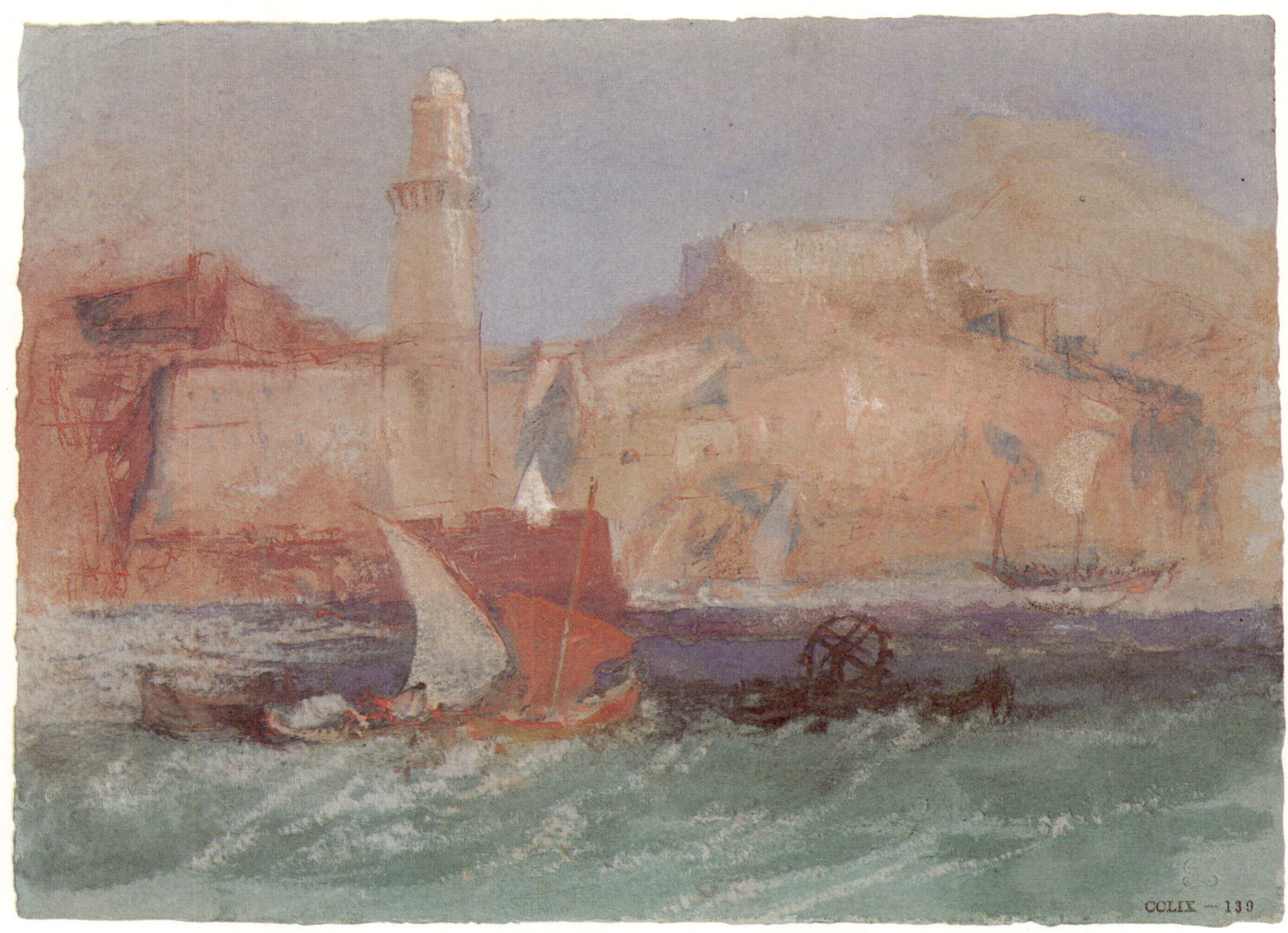

36 **The Lighthouse at Marseilles, from the Sea** *c.* 1830

pencil and bodycolor with scraping-out and some pen on gray paper, $5\frac{1}{2} \times 7\frac{1}{2}$ in. (141 × 190 mm.)

TB CCLIX-139

Although this drawing is on gray paper rather than blue, it is clearly one of the long sequences of studies made in connection with the "Rivers of Europe" project (see No. 34). The identification of the subject as Marseilles (cf. TB CCXCII-74) suggests that it was executed as a result of Turner's journey to Italy along the south coast of France in 1828. It may or may not have been made as a likely illustration for the work – it can hardly be said to depict a river; but it is in a comparatively highly finished state, with scraping-out and some penwork. At all events, despite the pencil underdrawing, it is most likely that Turner made the color study somewhat later than his visit to Marseilles: a number of pencil notes of the harbor occur in a sketchbook (*Lyons to Marseilles*, TB CCXXX ff. 52, 53) used on the 1828 journey. Several other sketches with similar rich color seem also to show scenes on the French or Italian coast between Marseilles and Genoa (see BM 1975 Nos. 149–58).

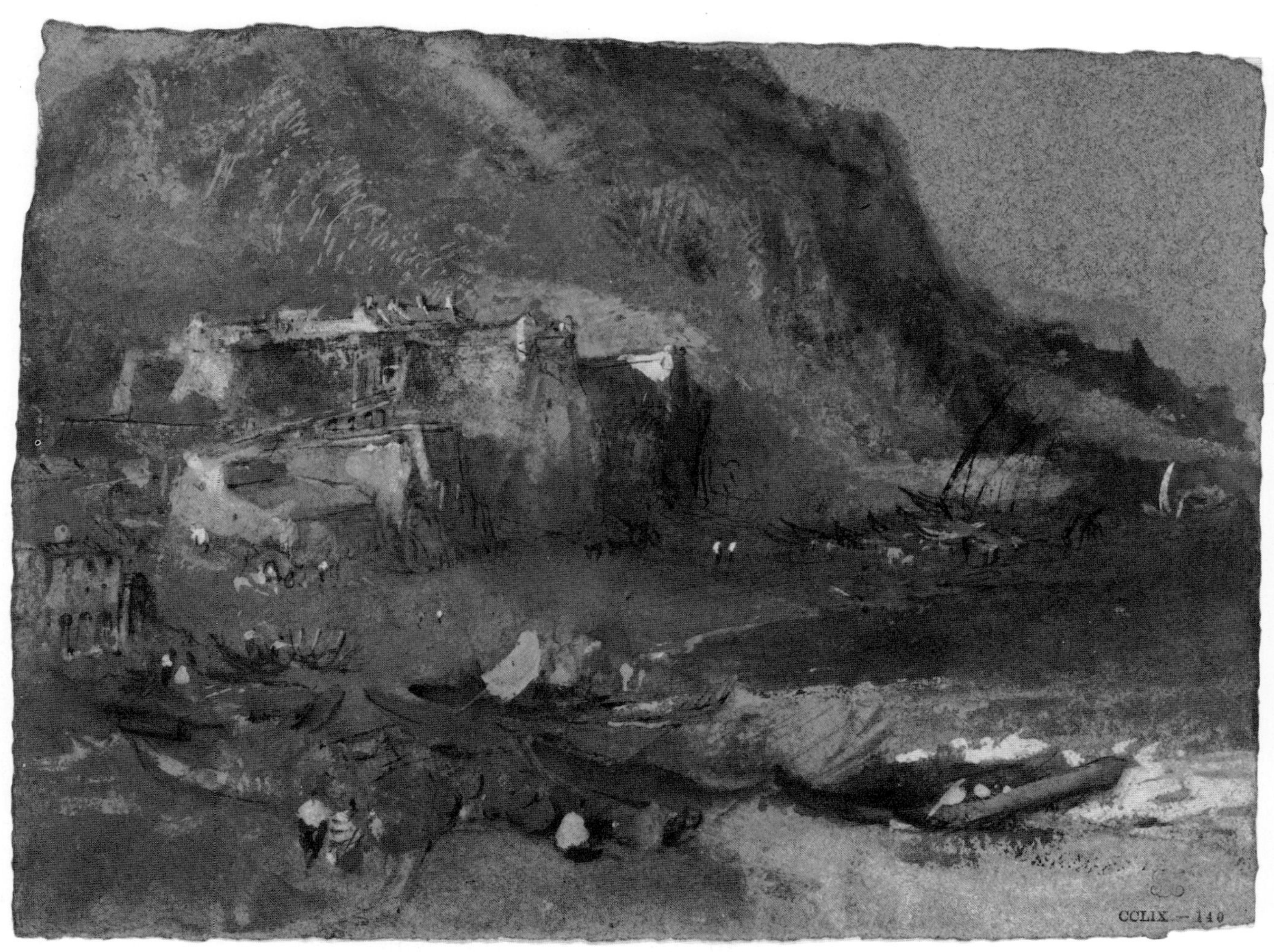

37 **A Village on the South Coast of France?** *c.* 1830

bodycolor with some pen on blue paper, $5\frac{5}{8} \times 7\frac{5}{8}$ in. (142 × 192 mm.)

TB CCLIX-140

The assumption that this drawing shows a village on the Mediterranean coast is based on its similarity of coloring to the view of Marseilles, No. 36. Turner was in the habit of making many color studies in quick succession, usually treating related subjects; but he may have employed the same palette in working up a number of topographically unconnected ideas taken from sketchbooks or from memory when he was planning the "Rivers of Europe" series. Many of the views which appear to show the Mediterranean share the general color scheme of the *Loire* subjects engraved in 1833, and were possibly worked up immediately prior to engraving; but it is difficult to place the individual sheets in the series in their exact chronological position.

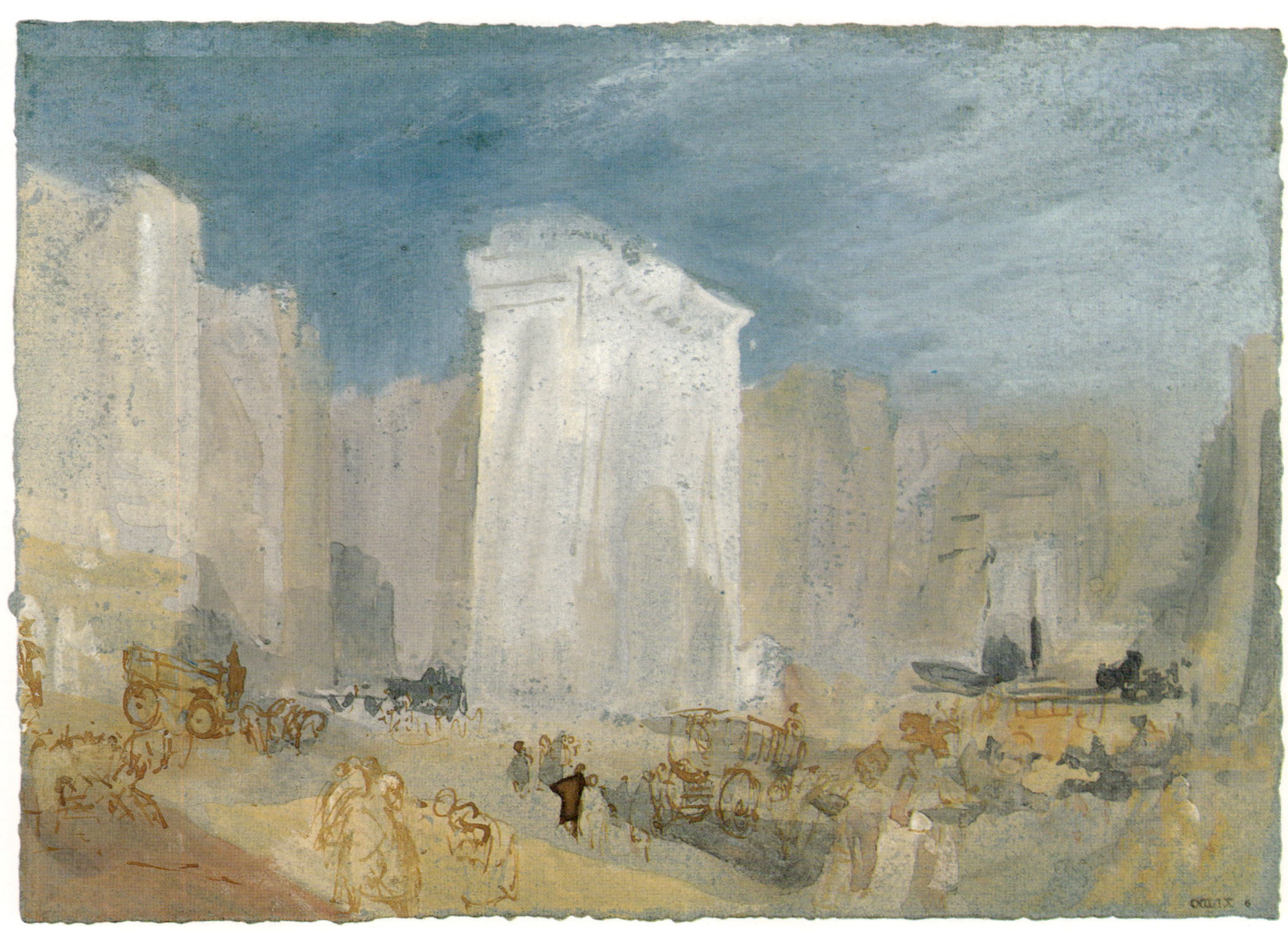

38 **Paris: The Porte St. Denis** *c.* 1830

bodycolor with some pen and yellow color on blue paper, $5\frac{9}{16} \times 7\frac{9}{16}$ in. (142 × 191 mm.)

TB CCLIX-6

Five views of Paris itself were engraved for the second volume of Turner's *Wanderings by the Seine*, which appeared in 1835 (the last of the three "Annual Tours" which were all that resulted from the "Rivers of Europe" project); no subject corresponding to this sketch of the Porte St. Denis appeared. Here Turner blocks in the principal feature of the view with the same bold generality that he would apply to the laying-in of an oil painting; the color-key is bright and rather chalky, a characteristic of most of the finished Paris subjects (TB CCLIX-117 to 120). This and the other preparatory or exploratory sketches on the same mat were presumably done from memory or from pencil notes after Turner's visit to Paris in 1829, though he went there again in 1833, the year of the publication of his first "Annual Tour," the *Wanderings by the Loire*.

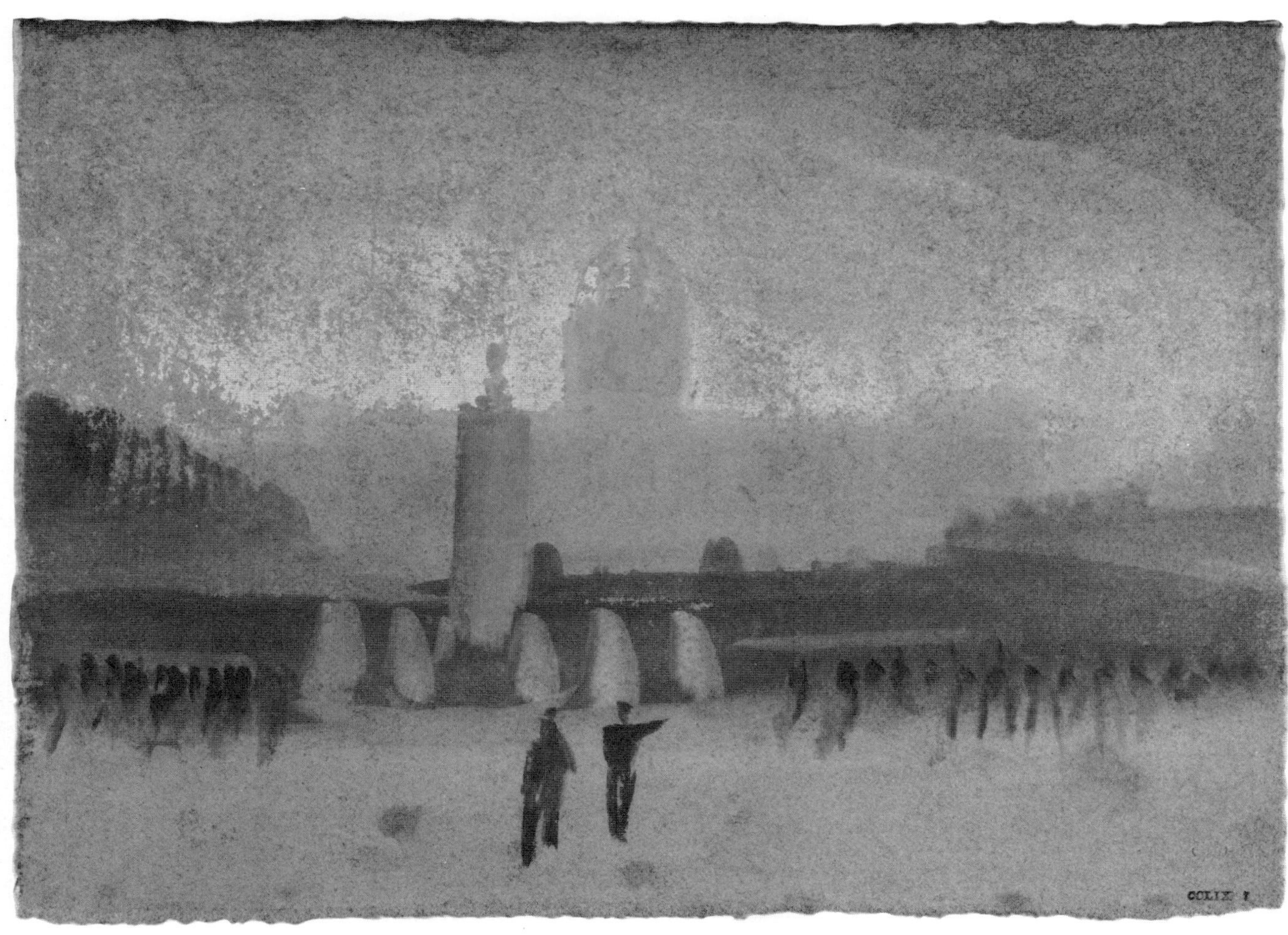

39 **Paris: The Invalides from the Champ de Mars** *c.* 1830

bodycolor on blue paper, $5\frac{1}{2} \times 7\frac{7}{16}$ in. (140 × 189 mm.)

TB CCLIX-7

Like No. 38, this is a mere beginning, an idea for a subject that Turner did not realize for the engraver. It nevertheless contains the seeds of a characteristically elaborate composition, with numerous figures bearing out the specific significance of the scene: the human activity indicated with a few black strokes in the foreground is evidently a military parade or similar exercise, illustrating the associations of both the Champ de Mars and the Invalides.

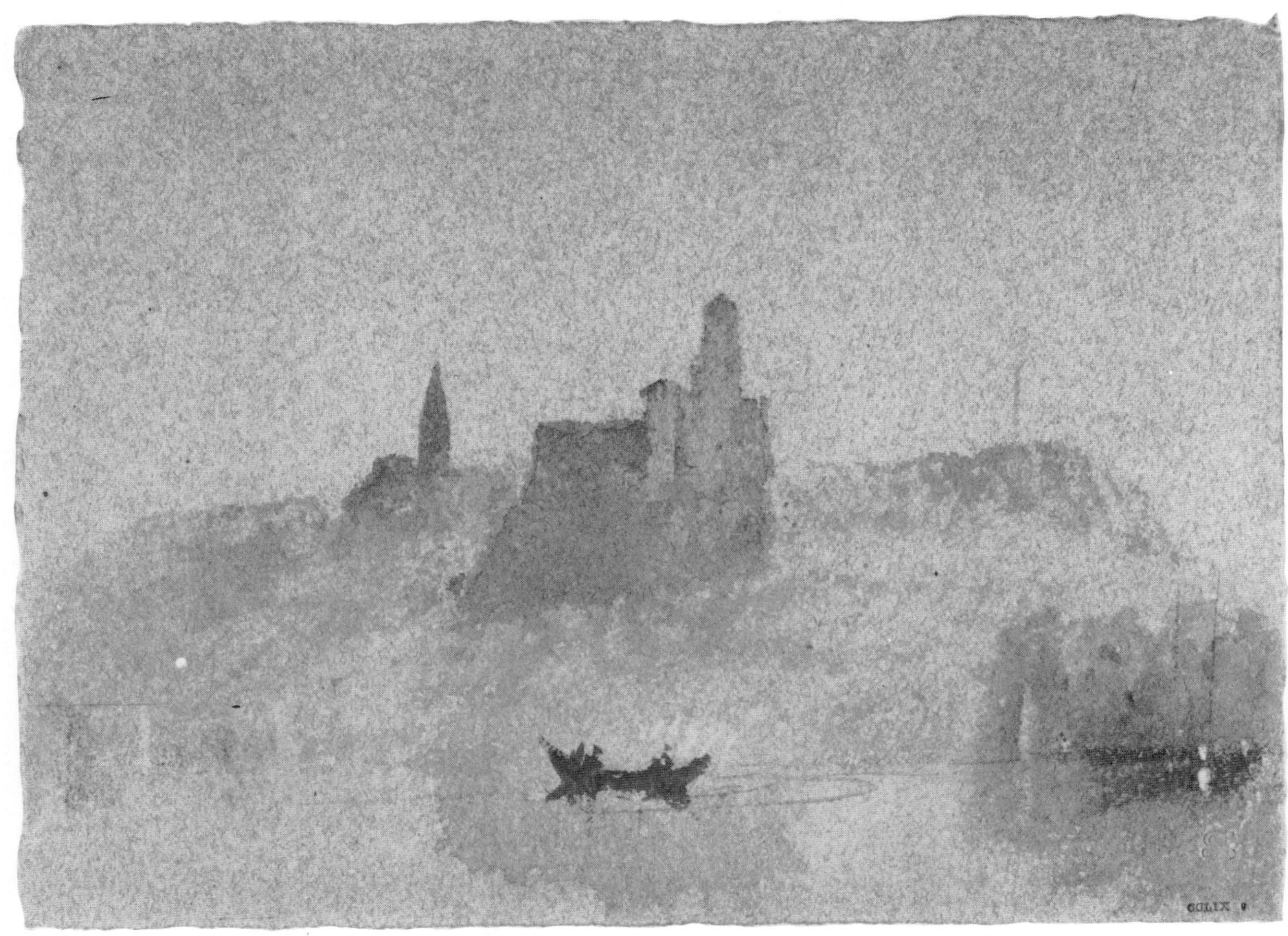

40 **Saint Laurent** *c.* 1830

watercolor and bodycolor on blue paper, $5\frac{11}{16} \times 7\frac{9}{16}$ in. (144 × 193 mm.)

TB CCLIX-9

This drawing was called *Saint Laurent* by Finberg, but is very similar to the plate of *St. Florent* which appeared in the *Wanderings by the Loire* of 1833 (R.446). Although it is not clear that the two subjects are actually the same – a finished drawing of the engraved version must have existed – the view here probably shows St. Florent-le-Vieil, between Angers and Nantes, which is presumably the "St Florent" intended in the title to the published view. In this case, Turner's delicate washes of pale gray and yellow on blue paper achieve a result that is complete in itself, but the drawing cannot be considered a "finished" design.

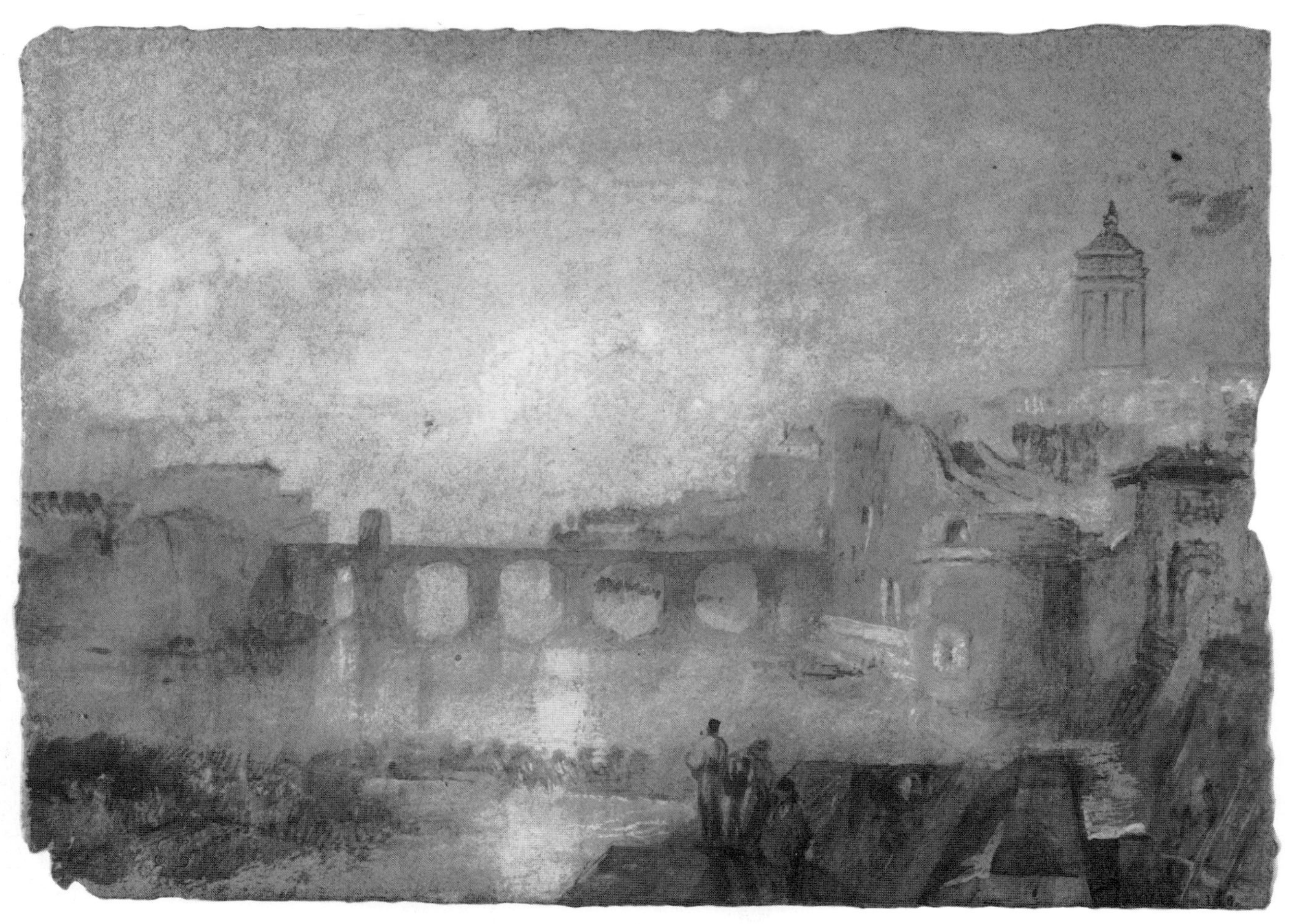

41 **A Town by a River with Bridge and Classical Monument** *c.* 1830

bodycolor on blue paper, $5\frac{7}{16} \times 7\frac{9}{16}$ in. (139 × 193 mm.)

TB CCLIX-166

This drawing has been brought to a high degree of finish, but was not engraved and, indeed, is rather enigmatic as to subject. The town depicted here has a slightly unreal atmosphere, and the great monument that dominates it, which should be easily recognizable, has not been identified. A similar structure appears in the view of *Honfleur*, TB CCLIX-182, but the present subject can hardly be that sea-port.

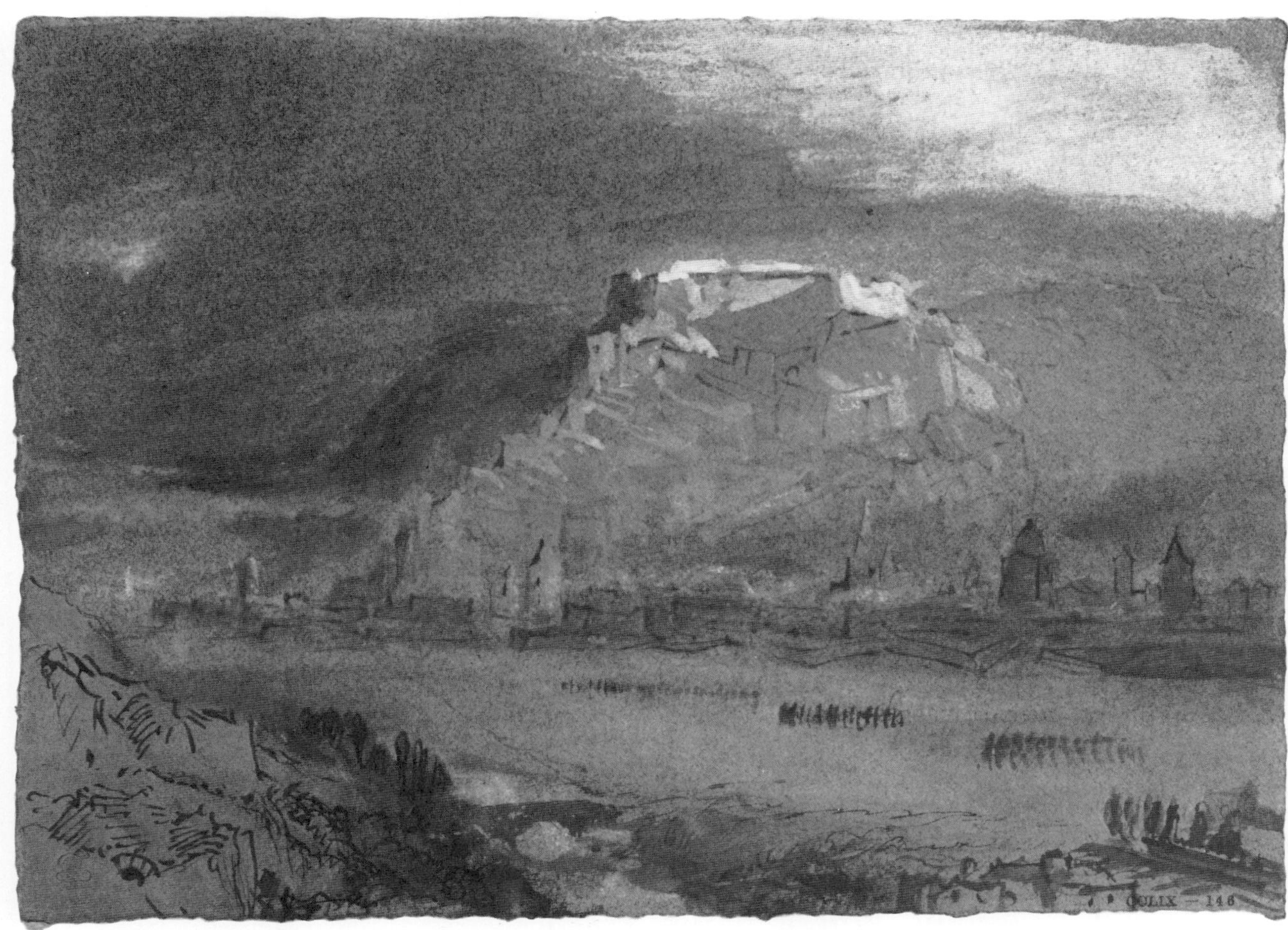

42 **Namur, with the Fortress Seen from Across the River** *c.* 1834

bodycolor with pen and brown, gray and green color on blue paper, $5\frac{1}{2} \times 7\frac{1}{2}$ in. (140 × 190 mm.)

TB CCLIX-146

Namur, with its dramatically sited fortress on a high spit of land between two rivers, inspired Turner to make many studies like this one (see also No. 43). Such forts are typical of the border land between France, Germany and the Low Countries, and were developed by Vauban and other engineers under Louis XIV; their elaborate piles of masonry with vast unarticulated walls and interconnecting galleries were for Turner fantastic palaces that seemed to rise organically out of the rock; he devoted much time to expressing these qualities, as they appear at Namur, Huy, Dinant, Luxembourg and elsewhere. In his studies they are nearly always presented as quasi-natural phenomena, without the commentary on their military function which so often occurs in other contexts (see the *Invalides from the Champ de Mars*, No. 39).

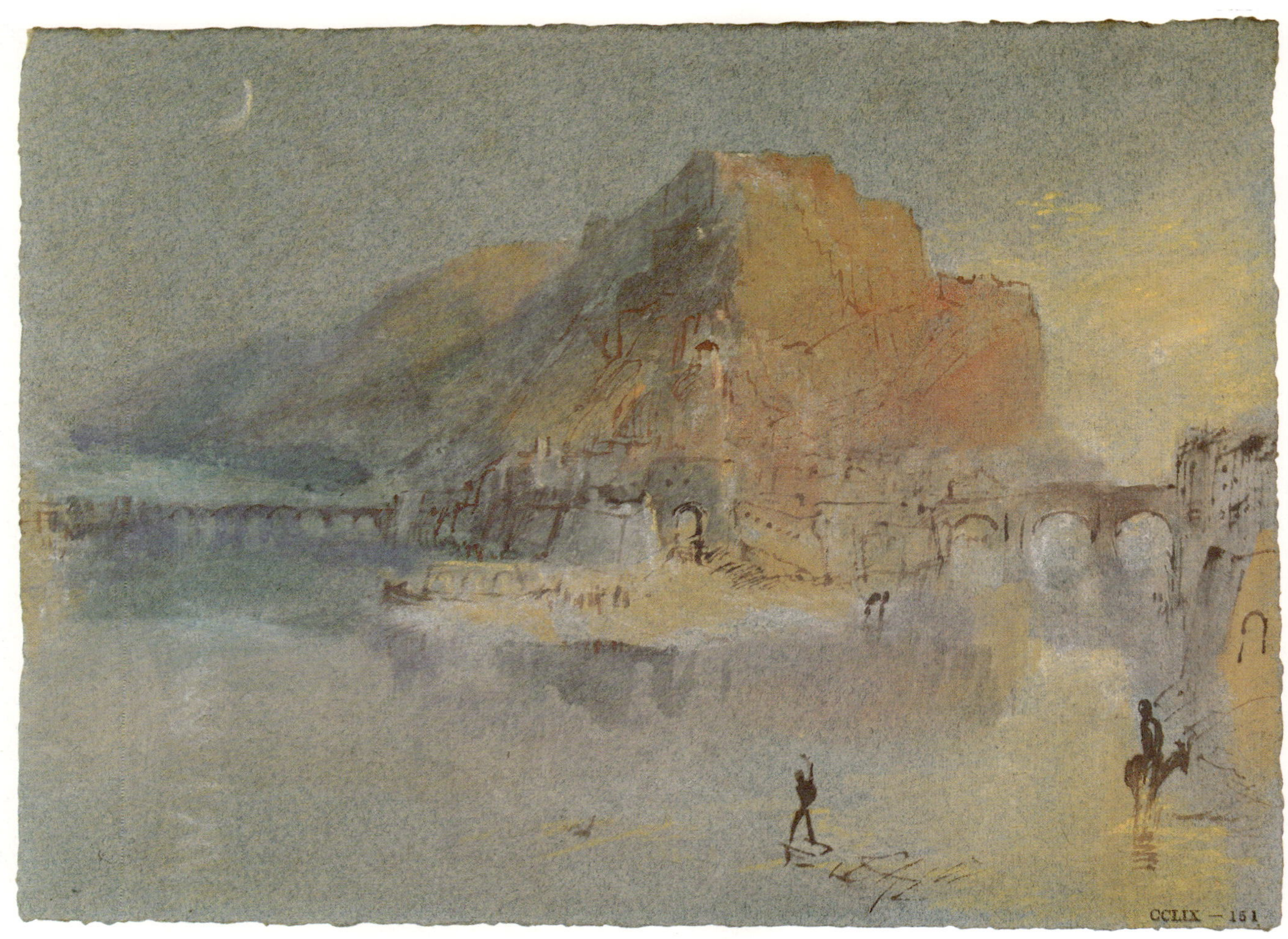

43 **Namur: The Fortress by Moonlight** *c.* 1834

bodycolor on blue paper, $5\frac{9}{16} \times 7\frac{1}{2}$ in. (142 × 190 mm.)

TB CCLIX-151

This is another study of the subject treated in No. 42. Both drawings were listed by Finberg among the studies made as a result of Turner's second tour of the Meuse, in 1834; the group that he associated with the first tour, of 1826, are TB CCXXI. There is no clear distinction to be observed between the two groups, and in any case Turner did not necessarily make such studies immediately after his tours: the drawings may have been executed considerably later. However, by about 1835 the whole "Rivers of Europe" project appears to have been abandoned.

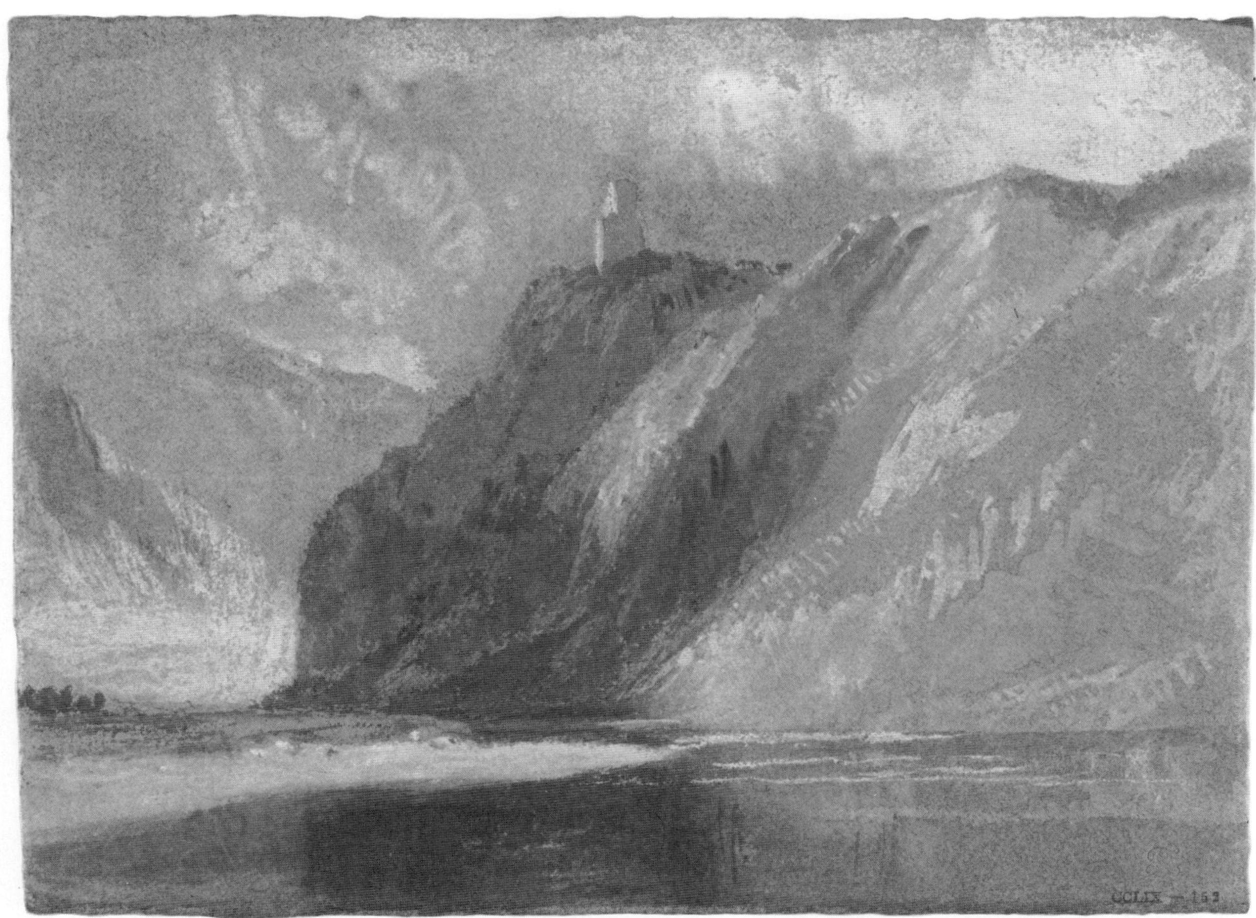

44 **Traben Trarbach on the Moselle** *c.* 1834

bodycolor on blue paper, $5\frac{1}{2} \times 7\frac{3}{8}$ in. (140 × 188 mm.)

TB CCLIX-152

This sheet was grouped by Finberg with the drawings made after Turner's 1834 journey along the Meuse, Moselle and Rhine (see No. 43), but, like others of the series, was possibly executed earlier. A slight sketch, washed with watercolor over pencil, showing the Moselle at Traben-Trarbach, is in the City Art Gallery, Leeds, and may have been made on the spot during the same tour. If so, it is possible that a series of similarly slight studies, also in pencil and watercolor on white paper, showing views on the Moselle and Rhine, can be dated to the same time. These are in several English collections, and there is an example at the Museum of Fine Arts, Boston. They have an affinity, also, with the airy and elusive panorama of *Passau*, TB CCCXL-3, and other drawings connected with Turner's journey along the Danube (also prompted by the "Rivers of Europe" project, no doubt) in 1833.

45 **Blue Hills** ?*c*. 1834

bodycolor on gray paper, $5\frac{1}{2} \times 7\frac{1}{2}$ in. (140 × 191 mm.)

TB CCXCII-72

A subject almost impossible to identify, and associated by Finberg (who gave the sheet its present title) with Turner's tour of 1834 to the rivers Meuse and Moselle, this study is on gray paper like the view of Marseilles, No. 36, and could equally well belong to the group with which that drawing is associated, or even to the series of drawings made after his earlier visit to the Meuse-Moselle region in 1826.

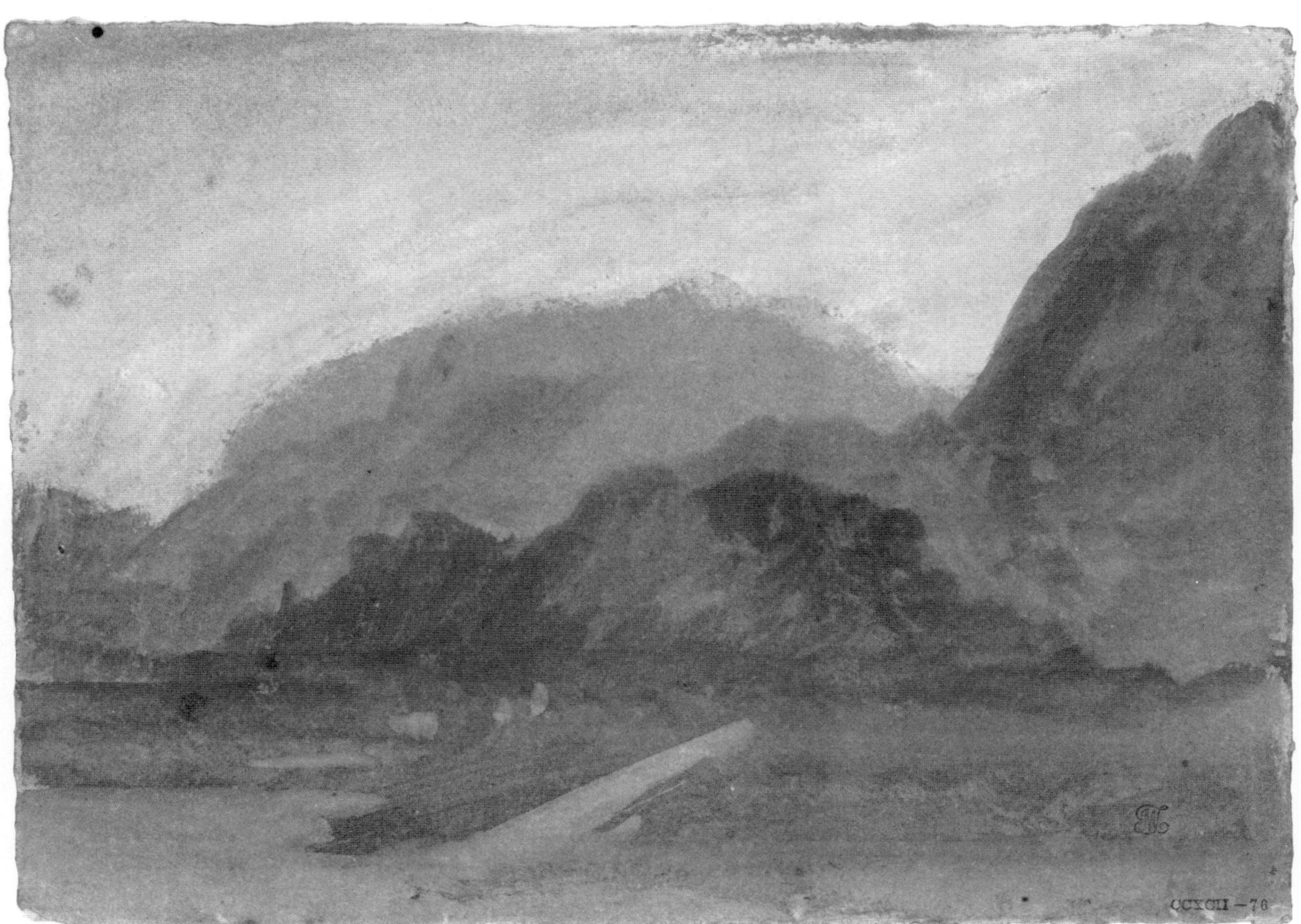

46 **Daybreak Among the Mountains** ?*c.* 1834

bodycolor on blue paper, $5\frac{1}{2} \times 7\frac{1}{2}$ in. (139 × 190 mm.)

TB CCXCII-76

The title given to this sheet is Finberg's; the study evidently shows sunset or sunrise over a town with fortifications and a castle on a height above it. The general feeling of the landscape suggests the topography of the Moselle, which would associate the drawing with Turner's journeys along that river in 1826 and 1834. Finberg placed it with the later group, but a precise allocation of drawings to each tour remains to be made. It is evident that, although these series of studies were probably a direct consequence of Turner's involvement in the "Rivers of Europe" scheme, not all the drawings actually show views on the rivers in question. Turner presumably experimented with a variety of views that interested him, regardless of their immediate usefulness in the context of that project.

47 **Study of the Burning of the Houses of Parliament** 1834

watercolor, $9\frac{1}{4} \times 12\frac{11}{16}$ in. (234 × 323 mm.)

TB CCLXXXIII-3

This is one of nine color sketches of the conflagration at Westminster which Turner watched on the night of 16th October, 1834. He made some slight pencil sketches on the spot in one of his notebooks (TB CCLXXXIV), but obviously conditions were not conducive to the making of elaborate records. For that reason alone it seems unlikely that these studies were made on the spot, though it has been argued that they were, on the evidence of the blotted color which appears on the backs of several sheets (including this one), perhaps indicating that he was working very rapidly (though the blots have recently been thought to be the results of much later damage by water). Turner might, however, have worked as quickly in his studio as he could have done out of doors, especially since the point of view changes considerably from one sketch to another, and the whole series has the air of a collection of general impressions organized as pictorial compositions, rather than of a set of records of circumstantial detail. Whatever his procedure, Turner made a more elaborate watercolor of yet another view of the scene (TB CCCLXIV-373), which appears to have been left in a state just short of completion. Two paintings of the subject appeared at the British Institution and the Royal Academy in 1835; they are now in the Museums of Philadelphia and Cleveland respectively.[1] In the same year a small vignette illustration of the fire, engraved after Turner, appeared in the *Keepsake* annual (R.323). The subject was one that fitted particularly well into the pattern of Turner's output in the mid-1830s, when he produced a number of other pictures and watercolors dealing with the theme of fire (e.g. *Fire at Sea*, *c.* 1835, Tate Gallery 558;[2] *Fire at Fenning's Wharf*, 1836, Whitworth Art Gallery, Manchester, D.100, 1892).

1. The Philadelphia picture is reproduced in Walker, 1976, pl. 23, p. 109; the Cleveland picture is reproduced in Herrmann, 1975, pl. 133, and in Walker, fig. 35, p. 35.
2 Repr. Herrmann, 1975, pl. 144.

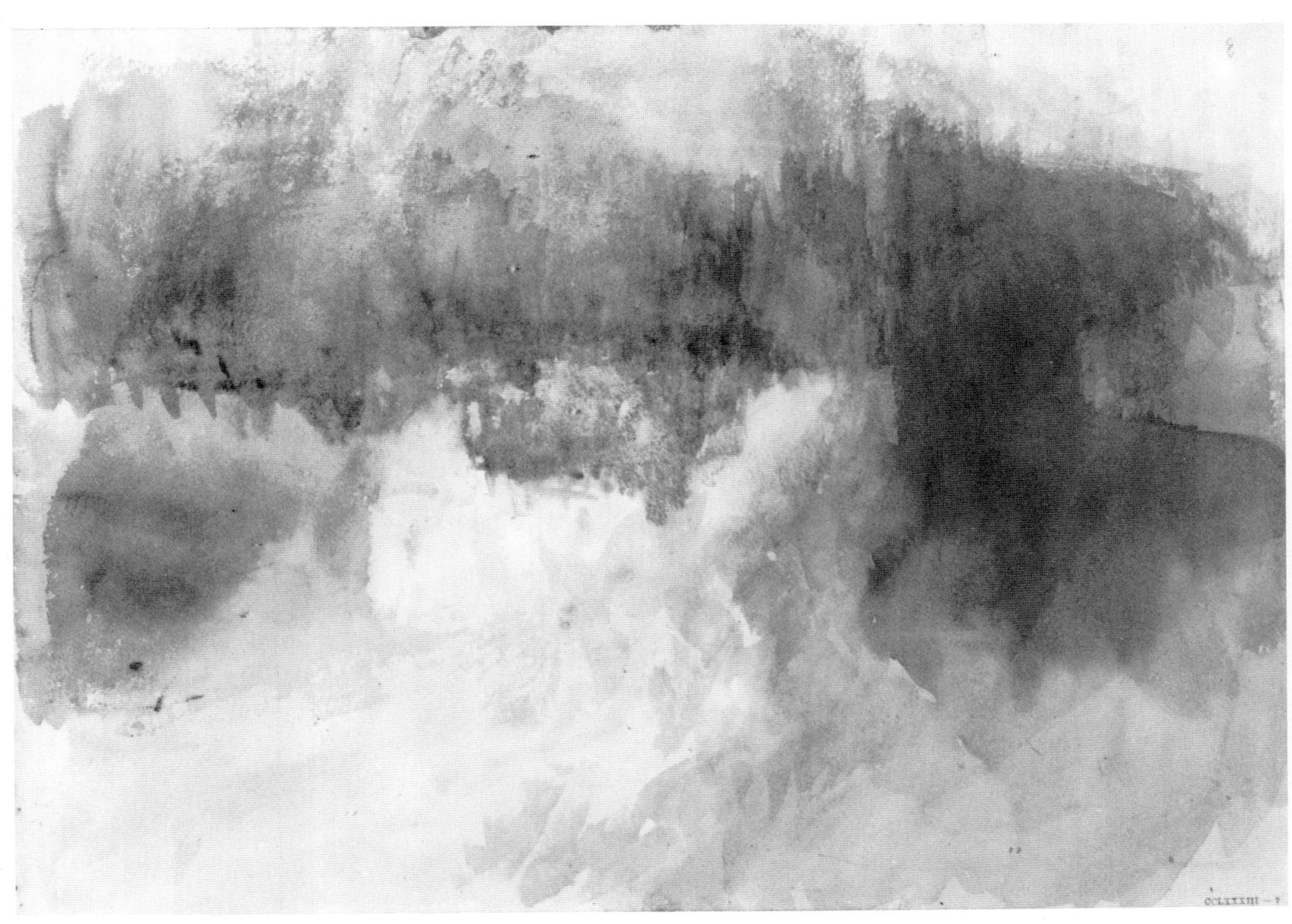

48 **Study of the Burning of the Houses of Parliament** 1834

watercolor, $9\frac{1}{8} \times 12\frac{3}{4}$ in. (232 × 324 mm.)

TB CCLXXXIII-7

A leaf from the same sketchbook as No. 47.

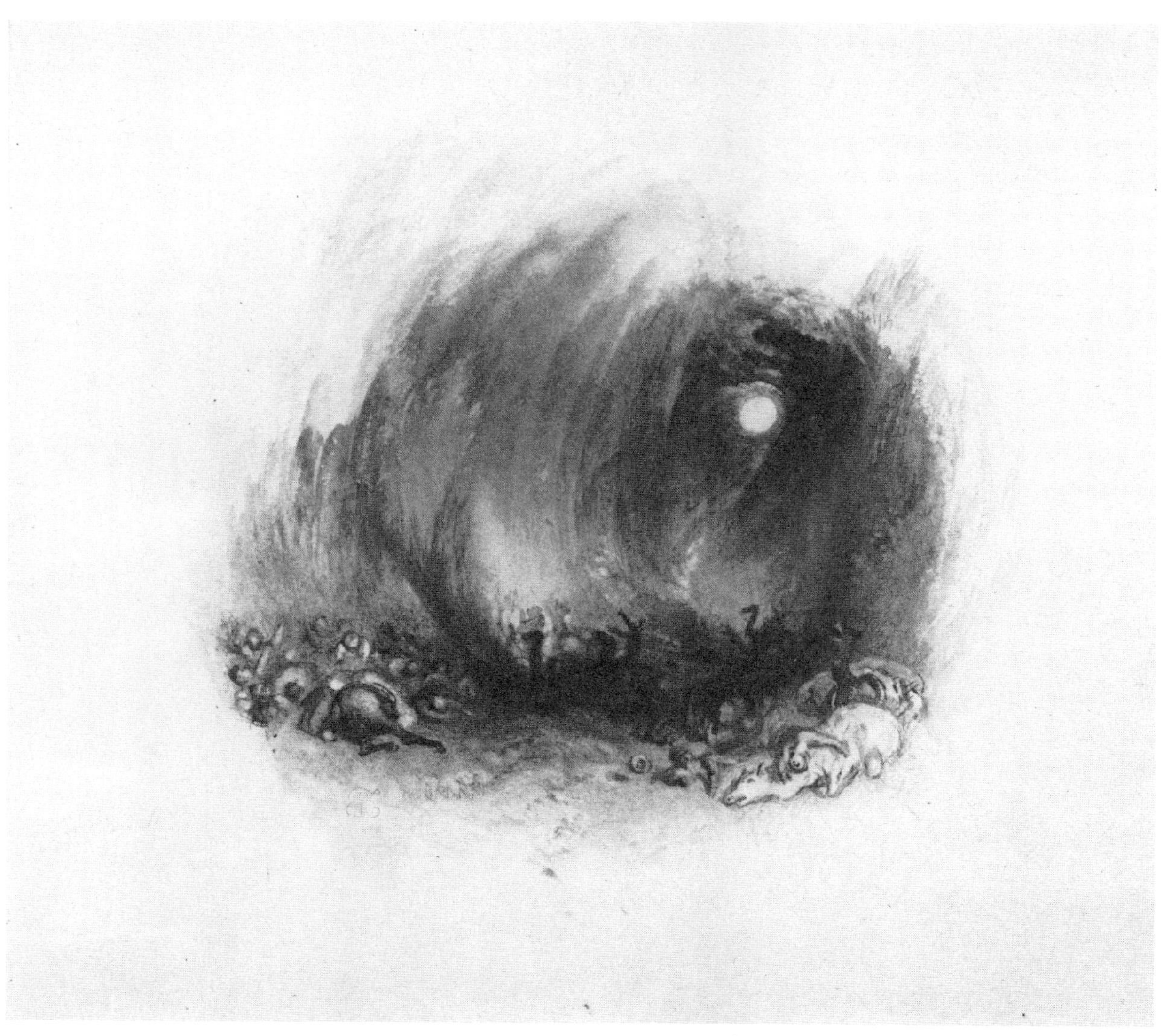

49 **The Simoom** *c.* 1833

watercolor, vignette approx. 5 × 5 in. (127 × 127 mm.)

inscribed above (not in Turner's hand): *Tail Piece*

TB CCLXXX-195

This is a finished design for one of the illustrations to Rogers's *Poems*, published in 1834: it was engraved by E. Goodall, and appeared on p. 94 (R.385, as *A Hurricane in the Desert*). Turner had already made designs for Rogers's *Italy*, which appeared in 1830; the poet, a friend of Turner's, had commissioned the work originally in 1826. The two volumes contain the most important group of Turner's vignette designs; he made others, together with a series of views, for the works of Scott, Byron, Campbell (see Nos. 53 and 55) and Milton, as well as for the Bible and a variety of other publications in the 1830s. This little drawing is a particularly impressive example of Turner's ability to concentrate vast forces and great scale into tiny space: the design is a reminiscence of the large painting of *Hannibal and his Army Crossing the Alps* of 1812[1] (Tate Gallery 490), and it anticipates, with its stormy vortex, the *Shade and Darkness – the Evening of the Deluge*,[2] shown at the Royal Academy in 1843 (Tate Gallery 531).

1 Repr. Herrmann, 1975, pl. 57.

2 Repr. Herrmann, 1975, pl. 151.

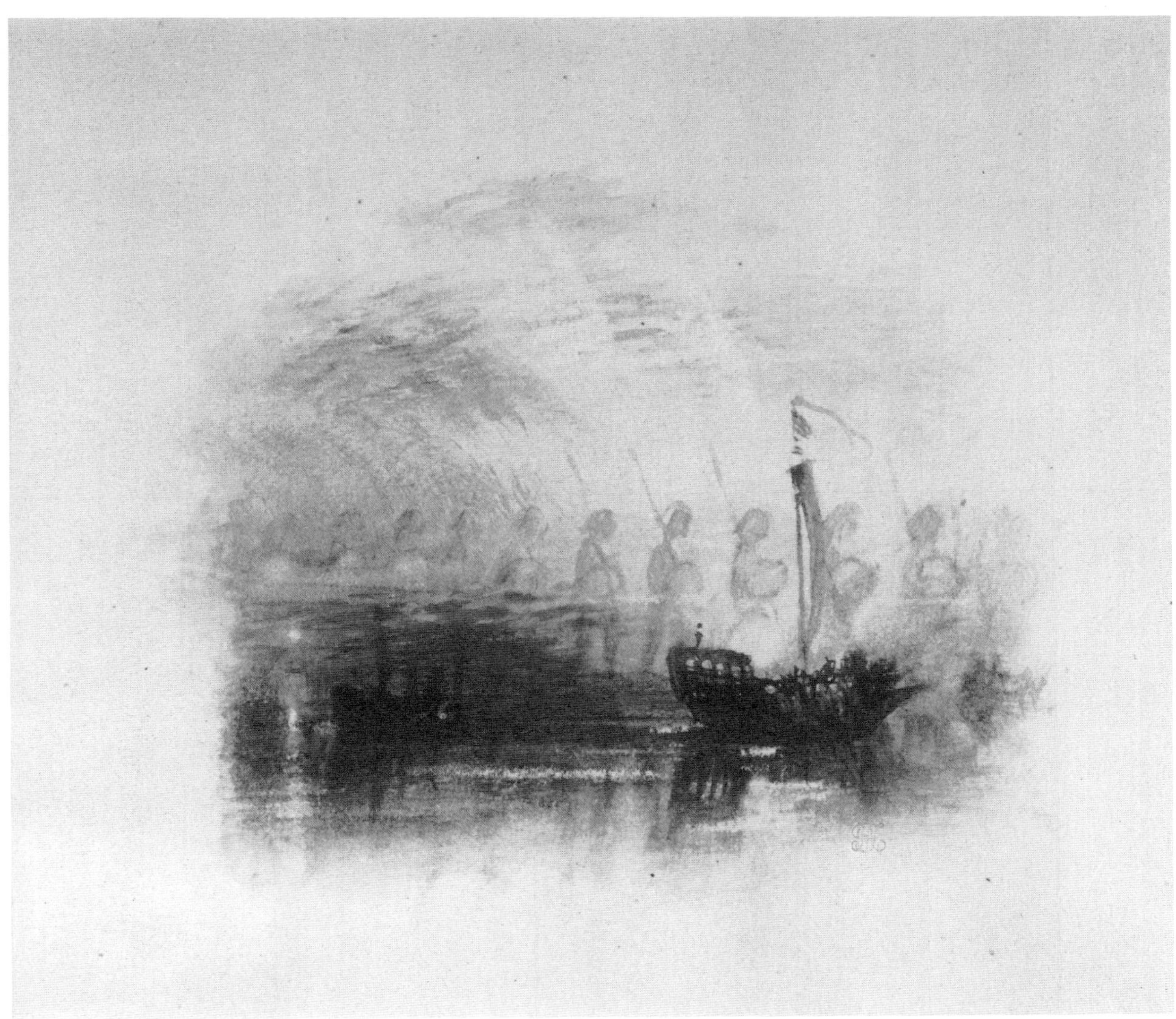

50 **The Vision** *c.* 1833

watercolor and scraping-out, vignette approx. $4\frac{1}{4} \times 5\frac{1}{4}$ in. (108 × 133 mm.)

inscribed below (not in Turner's hand): *Head Piece*

verso: a pencil study of the subject.

TB CCLXXX-197

This is the finished design for Rogers's *Poems* (see No. 49), engraved by E. Goodall and printed on p. 233 of the 1834 edition (R.400). The vignette illustrates the lines:

"... armed shapes of god-like stature passed!
Slowly along the evening sky they went,
As on the edge of some vast battlement;
Helmet and shield and spear and gonfalon,
Streaming a baleful light that was not of the sun!"

Two color studies for the design explore different aspects of the subject, combined in this final version. They are TB CCLXXX-203 and 204.

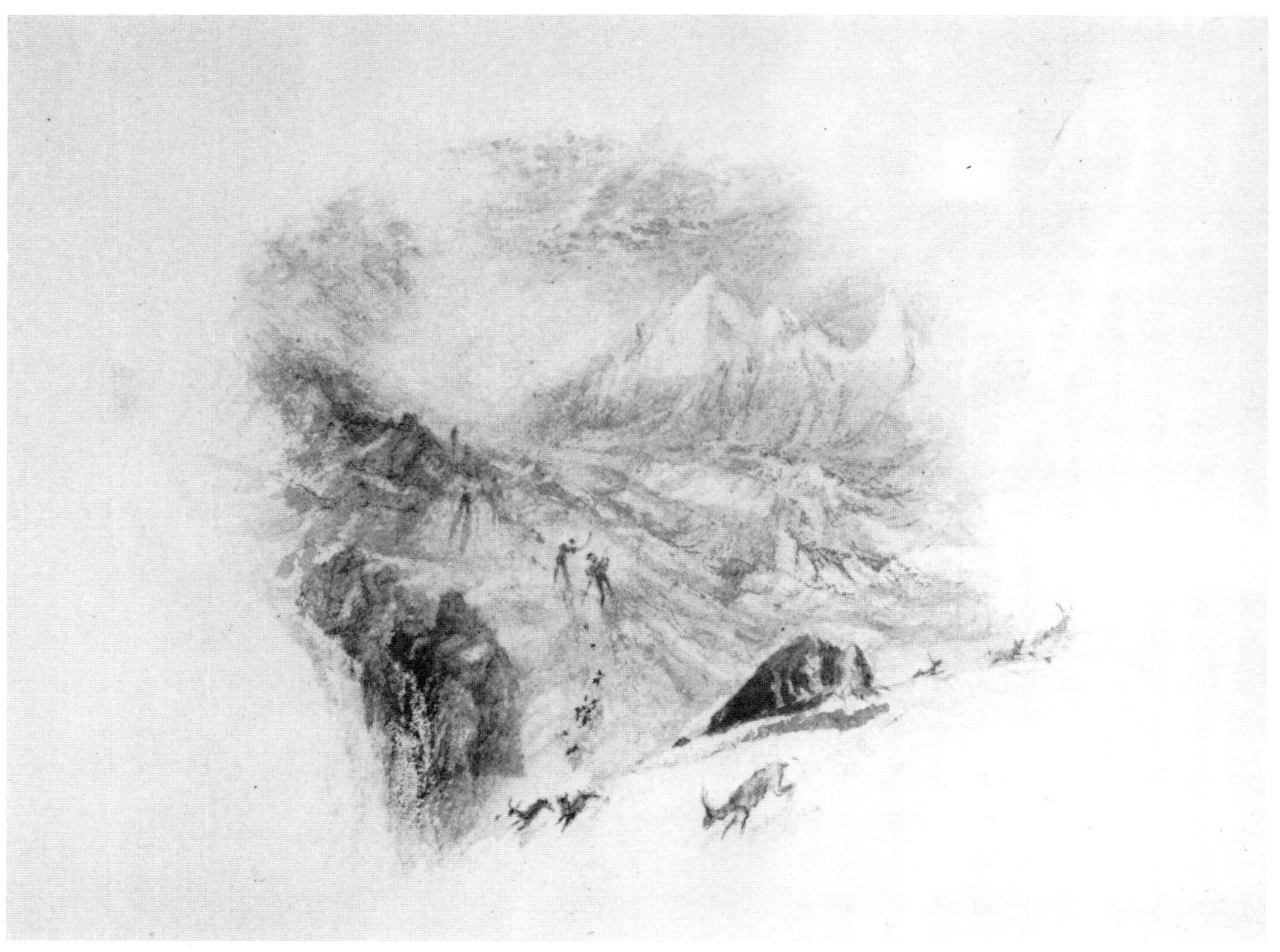

51 The Alps at Daybreak *c.* 1833

watercolor, vignette approx. $4\frac{1}{2} \times 5\frac{1}{2}$ in.
(115 × 139 mm.)

TB CCLXXX-184

This vignette, engraved by E. Goodall for p. 192 of Rogers's *Poems* (R.395; see No. 49), is one of Turner's most remarkable designs for illustration, evoking a huge expanse of brilliant landscape to which the white paper that merges with the edges of the subject contributes an impression of limitless and dazzling snow. In this very economical composition the deftly indicated figures, with their very specific movements and gestures, supply a reference point for the scale and atmosphere of the whole scene. Like *The Simoom* (No. 49), or the *Sunset* study (No. 55), the design is based on a vortex of light which gives dynamism to the subject and lends itself especially well to the characteristic format of the vignette.

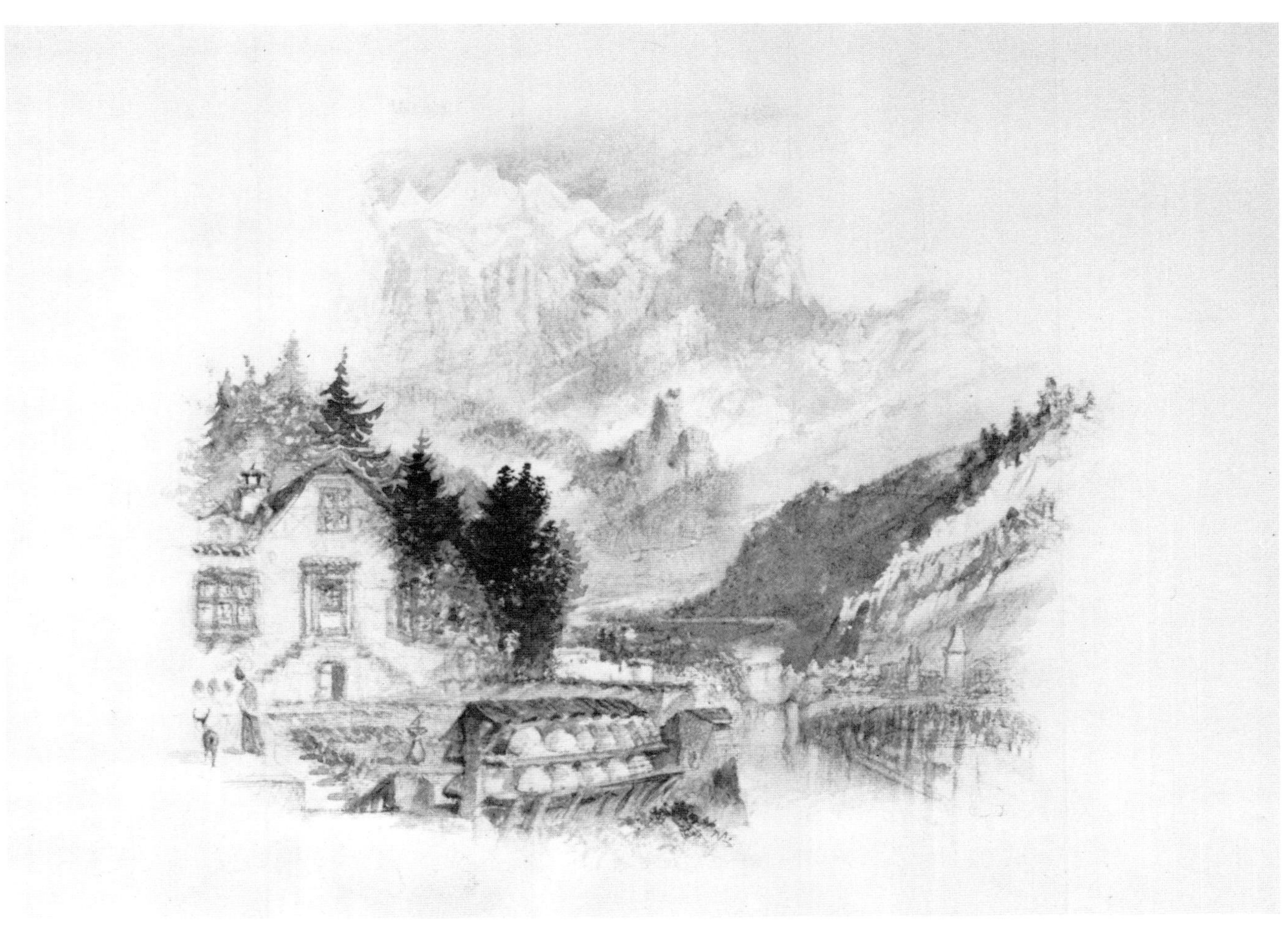

52 **Jacqueline's Cottage** *c.* 1833

watercolor, vignette approx. $4\frac{1}{2} \times 5\frac{1}{2}$ in.
(115 × 139 mm.)

TB CCLXXX-183

This vignette for Rogers's *Poems* was engraved by E. Goodall and published on p. 145 (R.388, as *St. Pierre's Cottage*). Turner's concern with the minutiae of his author's text is well shown here; he carefully delineates the details of the cottage and its garden, bee-hives, etc., while giving splendid breadth to the distant vista of the Alps.

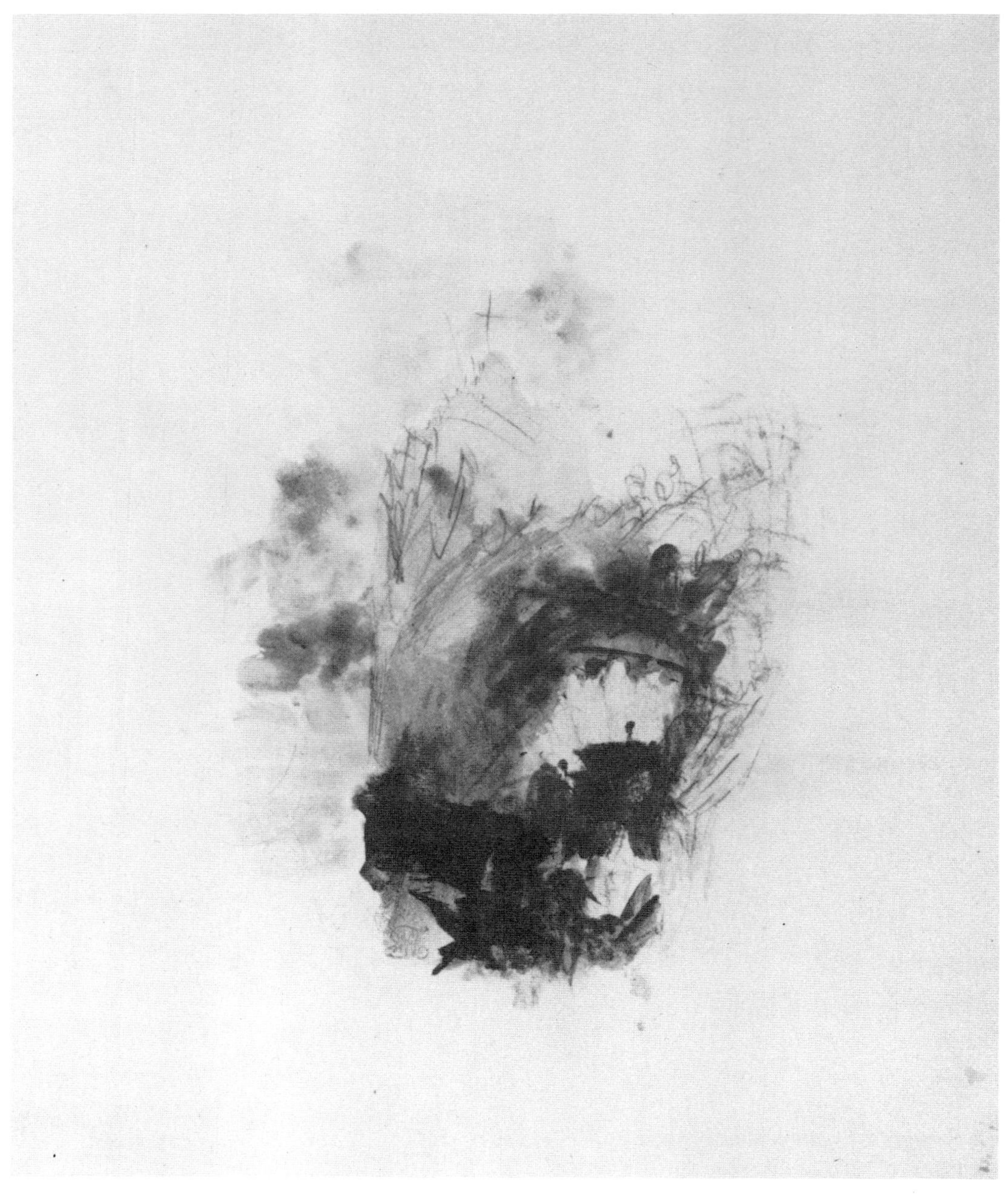

53

A Shrine on a Cliff-Top: Study for a Vignette *c.* 1835

pencil, watercolor and brown chalk, sheet $9\frac{3}{8} \times 6\frac{1}{4}$ in. (238 × 159 mm.)

TB CCLXXX-121

This study and No. 54 are obviously preparatory work connected with Turner's activities as an illustrator; they do not seem to incorporate ideas that were taken up in any finished designs, but in general style are perhaps closest to the vignettes for *Campbell's Poetical Works*, published by Moxon in 1837, and amongst the last designs of their kind that Turner made. These studies are drawn on thin card, which Turner frequently used while woıking on the vignettes; some small color studies which may be related to the *Campbell* illustrations occur in a little sketchbook, TB CCXCI(b) (see also No. 55).

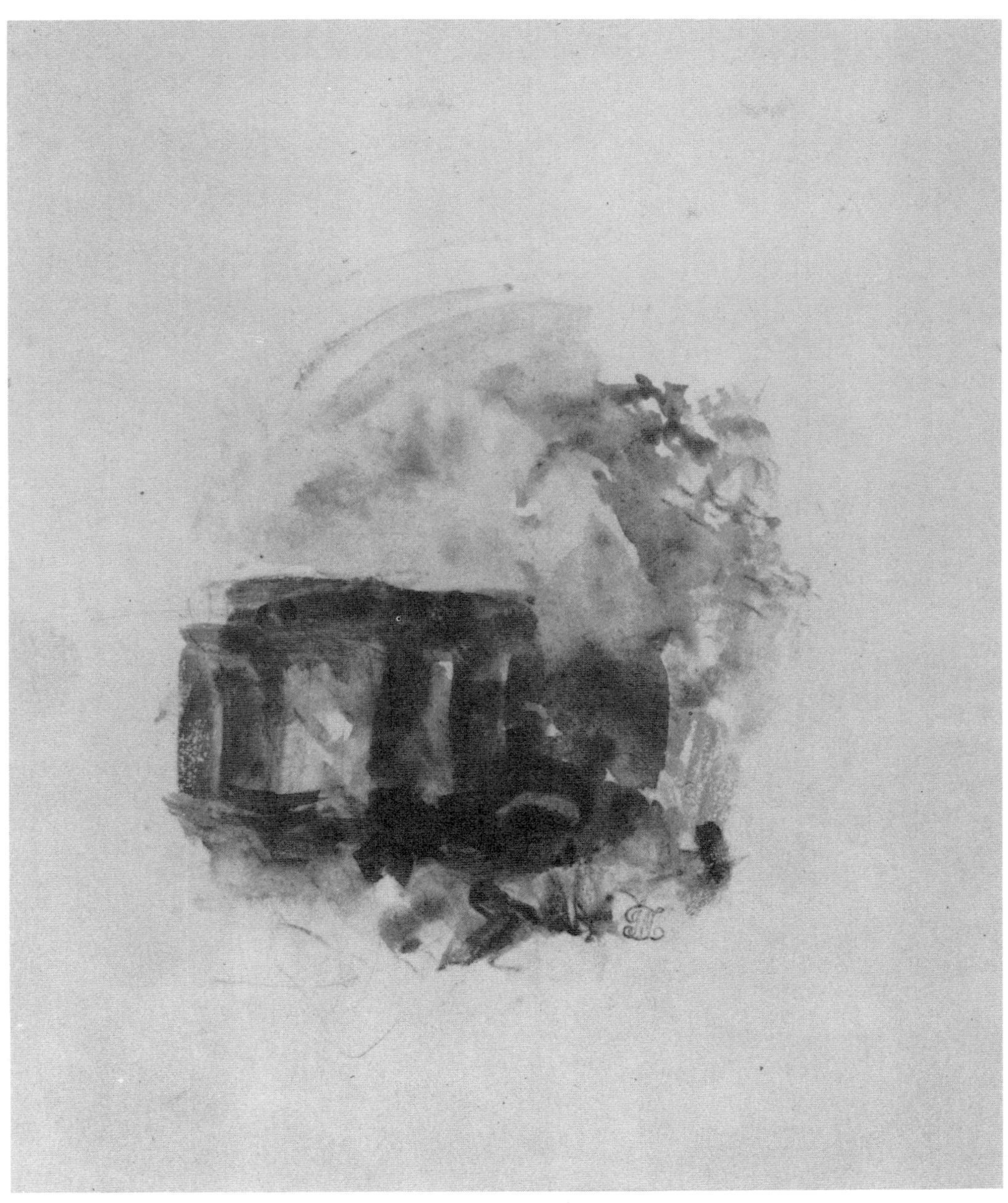

54

A Ruined Temple: Study for a Vignette *c.* 1835

pencil and watercolor, sheet $9\frac{3}{8} \times 6\frac{3}{16}$ in. (238 × 158 mm.)

TB CCLXXX-122

Like No. 53, this is perhaps a sketch for a projected design in the series of twenty-four vignette illustrations to Moxon's *Campbell's Poetical Works*, though there is no finished drawing that corresponds with the motif of the study.

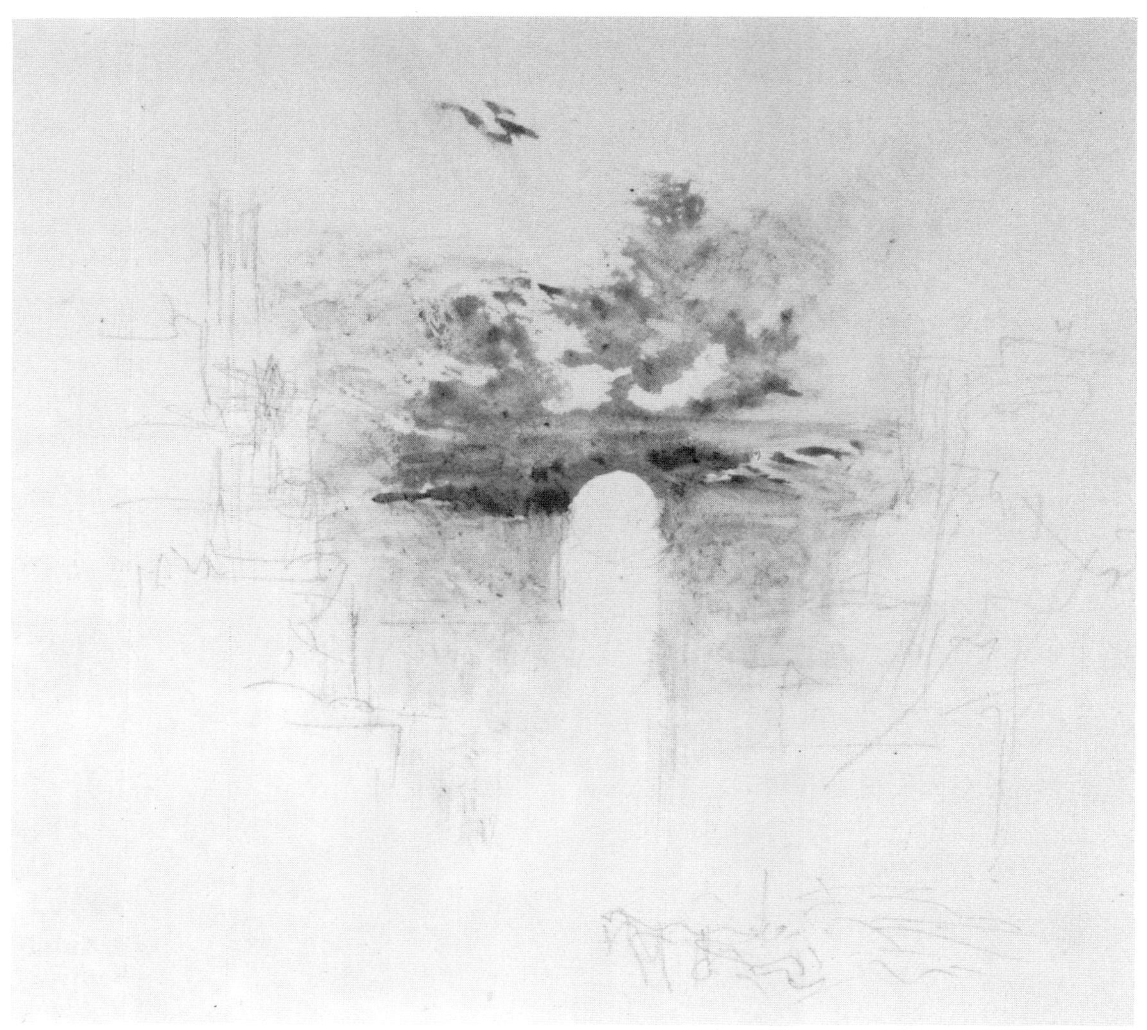

55 **A Sunset: Study for a Vignette** *c.* 1835

pencil and watercolor, sheet $8\frac{7}{8} \times 7$ in. (226 × 177 mm.)

TB CCLXXX-82

This is the initial color layout of a vignette illustration – possibly, like Nos. 53 and 54, connected with Moxon's *Campbell* of 1837, but not obviously related to a finished design. It may alternatively be connected with the illustration of "Tornaro" for Rogers's *Poems*, a large vignette of a sunset, TB CCLXXX-172. In that case both this and No. 56 would have to be dated about 1832–33. Turner's method of working here, in bold areas of contrasted color, corresponds exactly to the system that he used in planning much larger watercolors: the whole composition is reduced to blocks of elementary color. Whereas the two drawings, Nos. 53 and 54, have the appearance of exploratory sketches, this brilliant design might have been intended as the working basis for an elaborate finished illustration, with detail added in a mass of meticulous, fine strokes of the brush as in, for instance, Nos. 49 and 52.

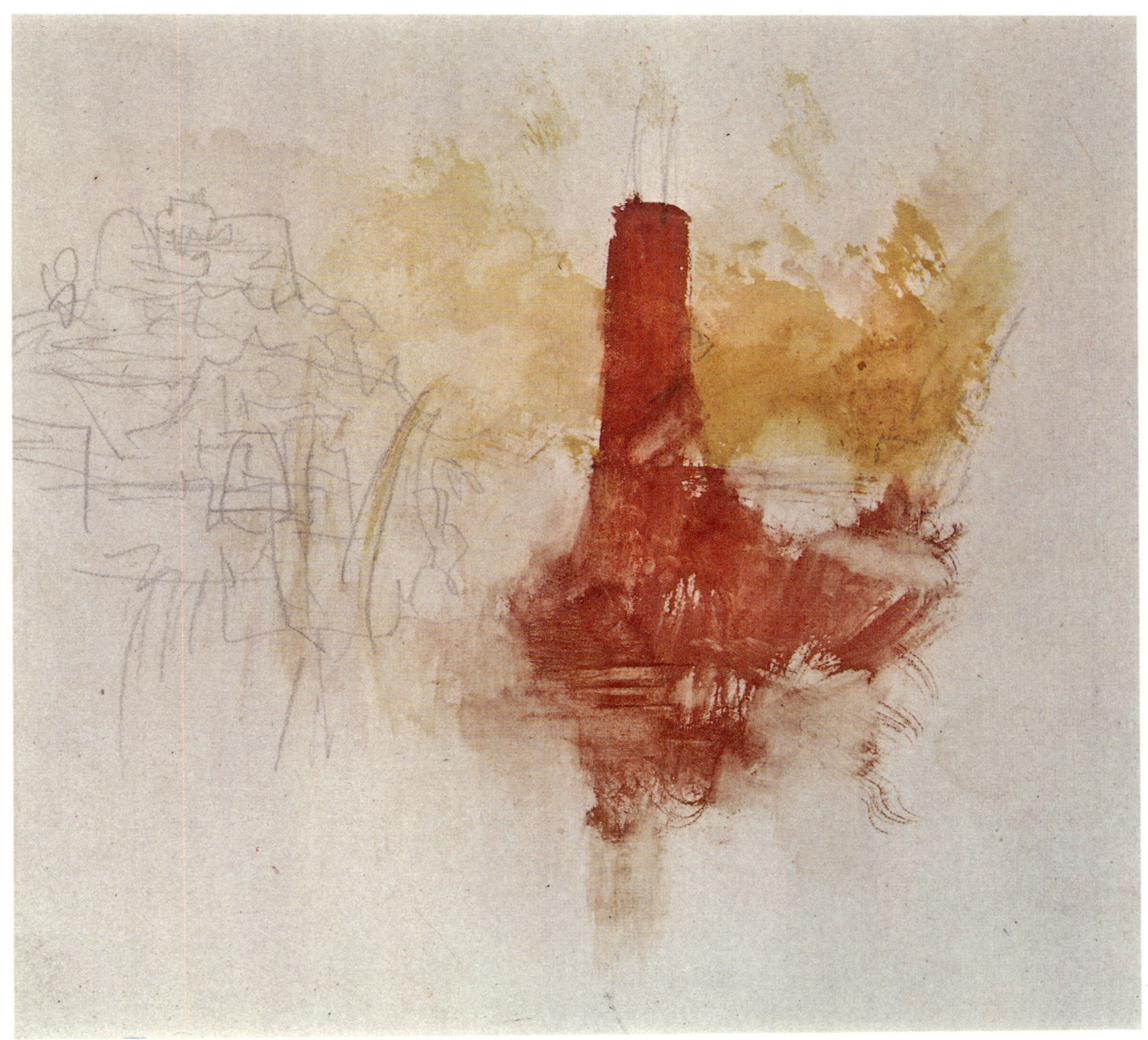

56 **A Scarlet Tower: Study for a Vignette** *c.* 1835

pencil and watercolor, sheet 9 × 6$\frac{15}{16}$ in.
(228 × 176 mm.)

TB CCLXXX-77

The comments prompted by the *Sunset* study, No. 55, apply equally to this drawing. Both designs draw attention to Turner's method of composing his small-scale illustrations: although the finished vignette was to be crammed with intricate detail, it was constructed on a very simple, single motif which gives it unity and dramatic immediacy.

57 **A Misty Shore with a Breakwater** ?*c.* 1835

watercolor, $7\frac{9}{16} \times 11$ in. (192 × 280 mm.)

TB CCLXIII-230

There are several drawings of this type in the Turner Bequest; some are on paper watermarked 1825, which provides a clue to their date, though such slight, atmospheric studies could have been made at almost any time after about 1820. A group of sea-shore studies in Ruskin's collection were called by him "scenes at Margate," where Turner spent much time, especially after he took a house there in the 1830s; these are possibly identifiable with a number of late sketches of sunsets now in various collections. It cannot be assumed, however, that a drawing such as this one was done at Margate, though it is very probable that it derives from Turner's experiences of the southern coast of England. It is likely to have been done in his studio, as a reminiscence of some observed effect, or even simply as an "invention." Turner painted a number of oil studies of the sea-shore between about 1830 and the end of his life; some of these, which imitate the broad, brilliant quality of watercolor, are associated with Great Yarmouth; his picture of *Life-Boat and Manby Apparatus Going off to a Stranded Vessel Making Signals (Blue Lights) of Distress*,[1] which appeared at the Academy in 1831, is a Yarmouth subject and a "public" expression of some of the themes of these studies, as is *Rockets and Blue Lights (Close at Hand) to Warn Steam-Boats of Shoal Water*, shown at the Royal Academy in 1840, and now in the Sterling and Francine Clark Art Institute, Williamstown, Mass. (it has been virtually destroyed by over-cleaning and repainting). A sequence of watercolor views of the sea at Yarmouth, more elaborate than the present slight study, but not "finished" works, is dispersed among a number of collections, including the Ashmolean Museum, Oxford, the National Gallery of Ireland, the Lady Lever Art Gallery, Port Sunlight, and the Yale Center for British Art (Paul Mellon Collection).

1 Repr. Herrmann, 1975, pl. 138.

58 **Venice: Looking Down the Grand Canal Towards the Casa Corner and Salute** 1840

pencil and watercolor, $8\frac{11}{16} \times 12\frac{3}{4}$ in. (221 × 323 mm.)

Inscr. lower left: *BAIDI* (?)

TB CCCXV-6

Of the many watercolor studies that Turner made of Venetian subjects, twenty-one occur in a sketchbook with soft covers ("roll sketchbook") which is watermarked 1834. This drawing is from that book. Most of the Venetian studies must have been made in similar books – Turner had begun to use the "roll" type in about 1826, and became increasingly fond of it – but the majority were disbound by the time of his death, and examples sold or otherwise dispersed. The 1834 watermark indicates that the book belongs to Turner's visit to Venice in 1840 (he was thought to have been there in 1835, but this date has been altered to 1833; see Hardy George, "Turner in Venice," *Art Bulletin*, vol. LIII, 1971, pp. 84–87); it was probably in use while he was there, but the studies were conceivably made afterwards, from memory, with the aid of his usual pencil jottings. A number of the drawings in the roll sketchbook, TB CCCXV, are of buildings on the Grand Canal, shown in soft, cool colors as in this example; but Turner's Venetian studies cover a wide range of expression, and vary from the most evanescent impressions to firmly stated and comparatively highly wrought watercolors, some of which he sold through his agent, Thomas Griffith. He did not, however, make any fully "finished" drawings of Venice, as he was to do in the case of Swiss subjects gathered in the following years (see No. 66); though he did produce a group of oil paintings inspired by Venice both after his 1833 visit and in the early 1840s; examples are in the National Gallery, Washington, the Metropolitan Museum, New York, and the Toledo Museum of Art.

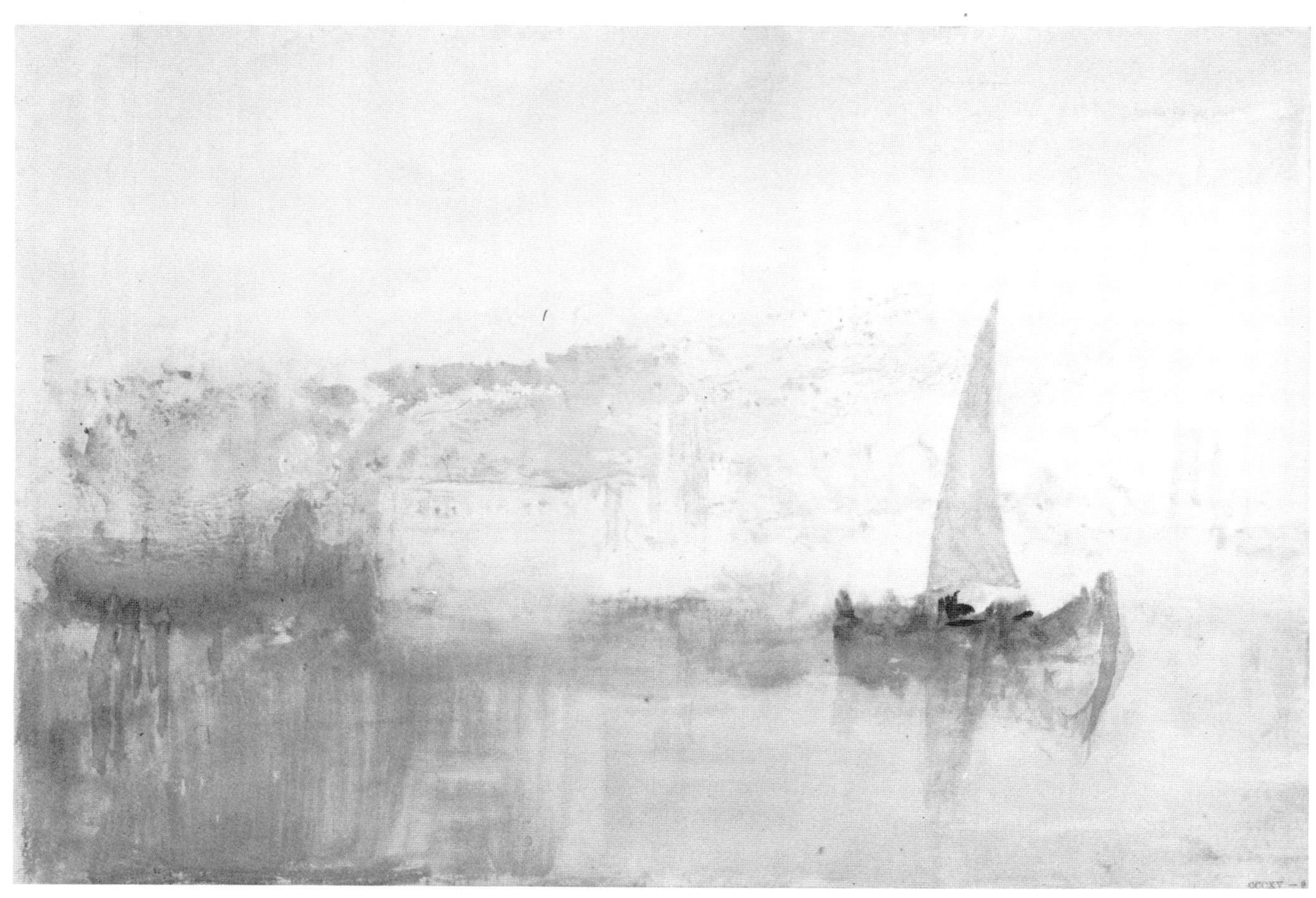

59 **Venice: The Riva degli Schiavoni with a Fishing-Boat** 1840

pencil and watercolor with some bodycolor, $9\frac{5}{8} \times 12$ in. (245 × 305 mm.)

TB CCCXV-9

Like No. 58, a leaf from the roll sketchbook watermarked 1834, this drawing nevertheless seems to belong to a different "sequence" among the Venetian studies; its combination of salmon-pink and green recurs in various examples from the disbound books. There can be little doubt that, as was so often the case, Turner worked on his Venetian drawings in groups, executed together as sets of "variations" on particular combinations of colors; but whether he did so using several books simultaneously or working steadily through one book after another is not clear. The drawings themselves often seem to provide evidence that he turned from one book to another – perhaps to save time while color was drying; he certainly made most of the studies away from the motif, presumably at his hotel (the Europa, at the mouth of the Grand Canal, opposite the Dogana).

60 **Venice: Distant View of the Entrance to the Grand Canal** 1840

watercolor on off-white paper, $9\frac{1}{16} \times 11\frac{15}{16}$ in. (230 × 303 mm.)

TB CCCXVI-13

This is one of five Venetian drawings in the Turner Bequest which are not on the usual smooth white Whatman or similar paper. They make use of a coarser, slightly creamy paper which Turner exploits to create slightly blurred, misty images, as of the city seen through early morning haze or evening twilight. In this study we are reminded of the economical freshness of the watercolors he made on his first visit (see No. 11), but this is a more schematic, generalized account, less a record of how Venice appears, than of the emotional effect created by its vast arenas of reflected and diffused light. We may well conclude from examples like this that Turner was working at some distance from his original, perhaps, even, after his return to London.

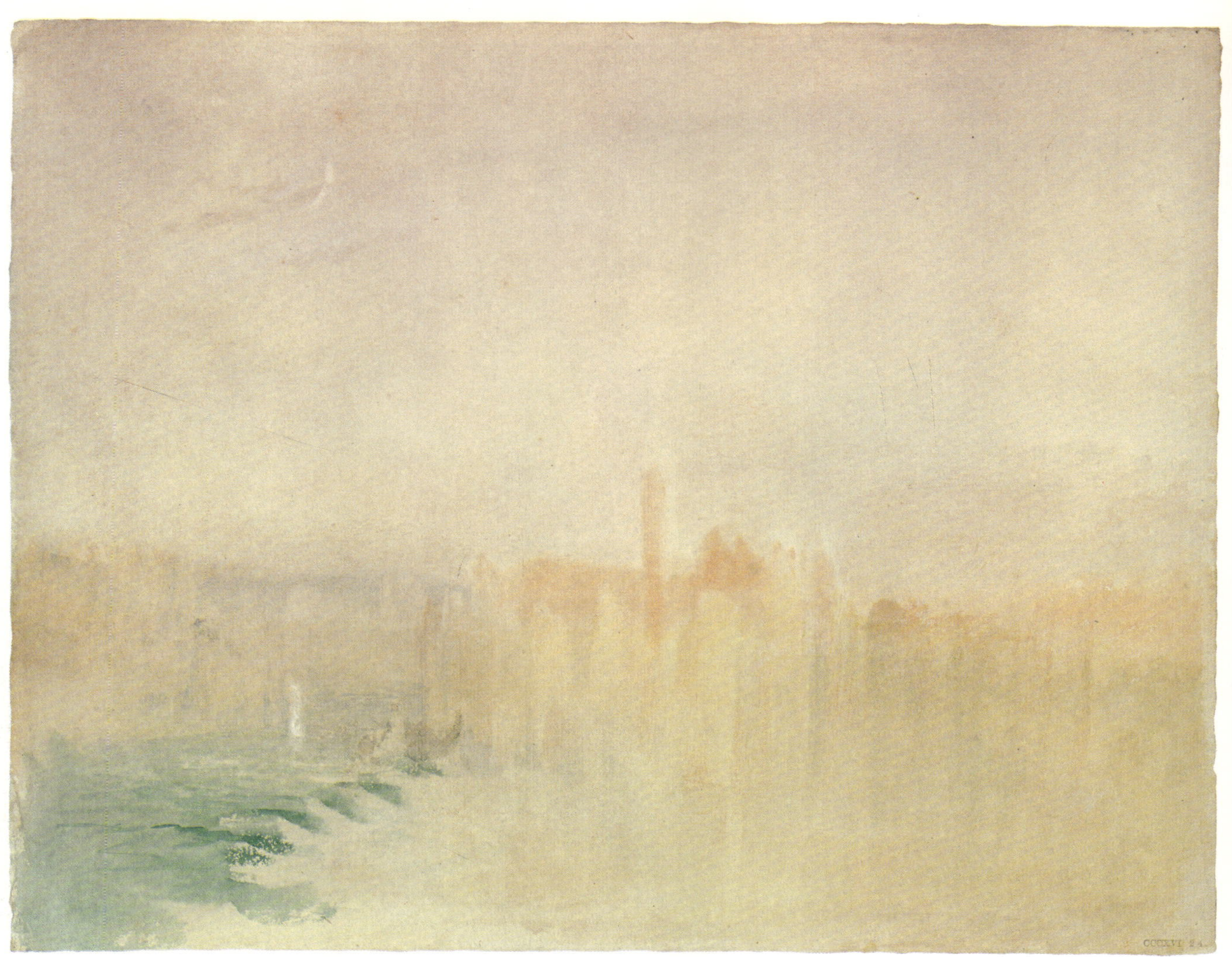

61 **Venice: S. Giorgio Maggiore at Sunset** 1840

watercolor, $9\frac{9}{16}$ × 12 in. (243 × 306 mm.)

TB CCCXVI-24

This sheet is a ravishing example of Turner's ability to generalize and intensify the emotional significance of a specific view: we are conscious here of a stripping away of detail in the interest of vivid poetic effect. Colors of great richness are combined inventively in a very simple scheme of blocks of mauve, green, yellow, and blue around the central strip of salmon-orange. Studies of this type were probably made concurrently with more literally factual ones such as those of the buildings on the Grand Canal (see No. 58); indeed, we can see similar groups of colors used in both types, but in contrasting ways to very different ends (see *The Arsenal*, No. 63).

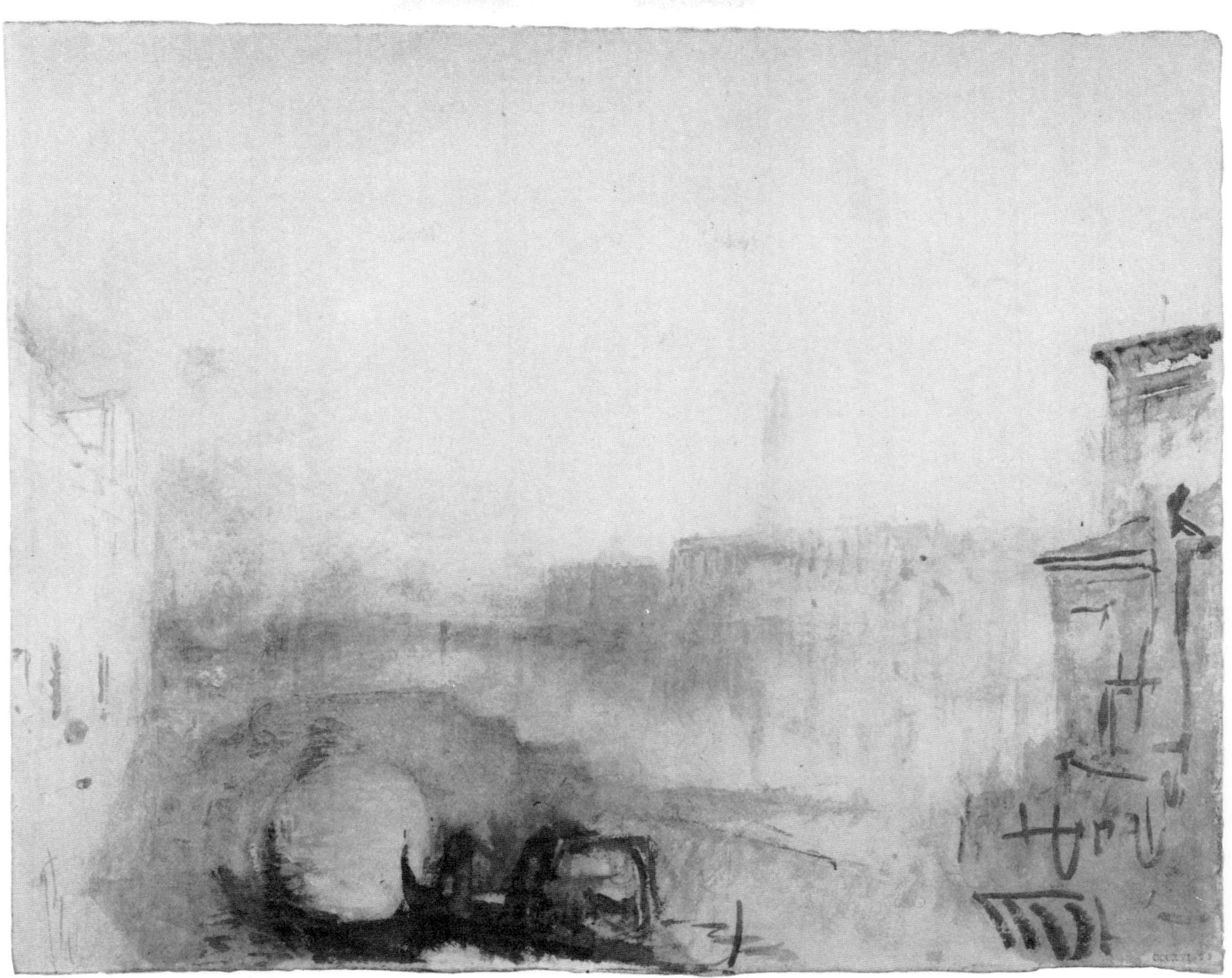

62 **Venice: Looking West Towards the Salute and Doges' Palace with the Campanile of St. Mark's Beyond** 1840

watercolor, $9\frac{9}{16}$ × 12 in. (243 × 304 mm.)

TB CCCXVI-23

Very different in its approach and mood from Nos. 59 and 61, this drawing displays a coarser, less precise touch in almost all its details. The central distance is worked up with loose, vigorous strokes over the customary broad washes, while in the architectural detail of the building at the right, Turner uses the most summary strokes of a brush dipped in black color. Similar coarse handling can be found in other examples from the Venice series, e.g. TB CCCXV-13, CCCXVI-16, 21 (note that these do not all come from the same sketchbook). Despite this apparent perfunctoriness, the whole view has the luminosity that is characteristic of these drawings, making use, as they do to an unparalleled degree, of the whiteness of the paper to achieve an effect of all-pervasive light. This device was something that Turner tried to reproduce in many of the oil paintings that he executed in the last decades of his life, working on a light ground instead of the dark tone of traditional practice. He had himself experimented with a white ground for oil paintings in the series of studies that he made along the Thames in the first decade of the century (see No. 8); it became increasingly common in his pictures from the 1820s onwards.

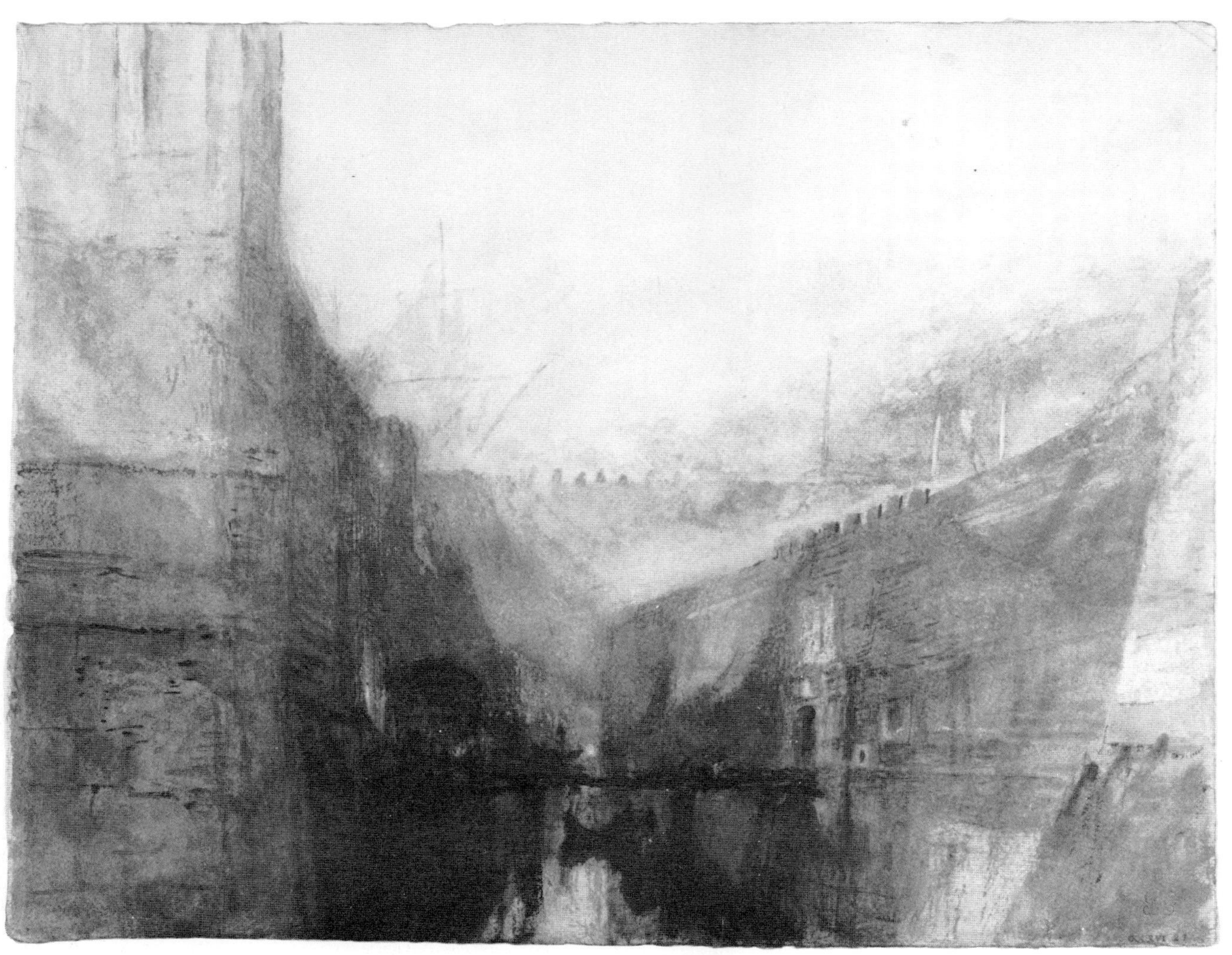

63 **Venice: The Arsenal** 1840

watercolor, $9\frac{1}{2} \times 12\frac{1}{8}$ in. (242 × 307 mm.)

verso: pencil studies of figures, horses and carts

TB CCCXVI-27

This drawing is somewhat unusual among the Venetian studies on white paper (Turner made a sequence of Venice views on brown paper, TB CCCXVII, which include interiors) in being dominated by an architectural feature rather than by the open spaces of the Grand Canal, Bacino and Lagoon. Even so, it seems to belong to the same series as the view of *S. Giorgio Maggiore at Sunset* (No. 61), for it shares with that drawing the same palette of salmony-orange, mauve and yellow. It is typical of Turner that the same group of colors should be employed in a totally different context to achieve a very dissimilar effect. No doubt the artist was thinking of the impressive architectural perspectives of Piranesi when he made this brooding study – it has little in common with the "topographical" interiors that he himself made in the 1790s, when he had already certainly come into contact with Piranesi's prints; a watercolor copy by him of one of them, dating from about 1795, is in the Metropolitan Museum, New York.[1]

1 Repr. Berkeley, 1975, No. 4, p. 73.

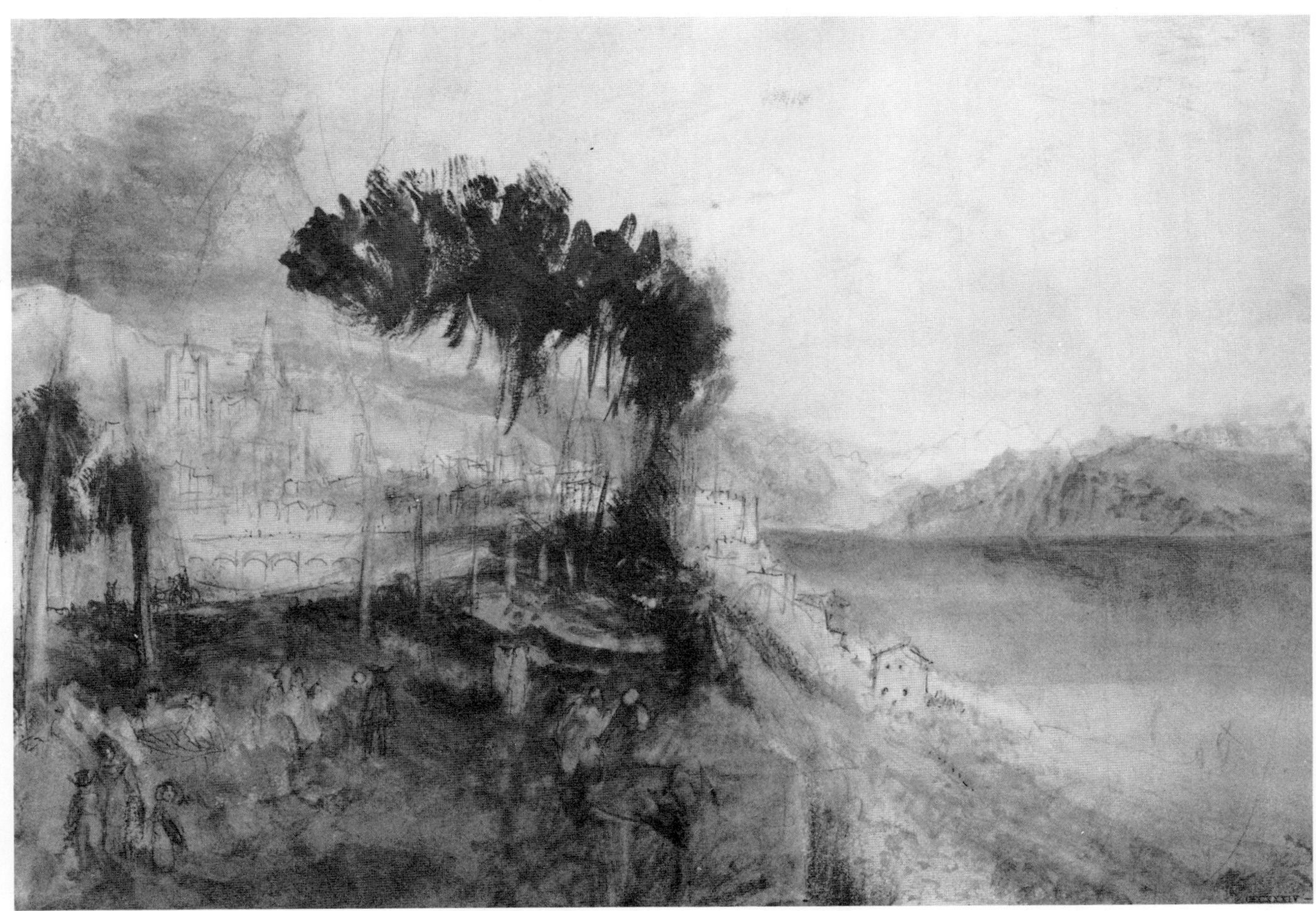

64 **Lausanne with the Lake of Geneva, Looking East** 1841

pencil and watercolor with pen and red ink, $9\frac{1}{8} \times 13\frac{1}{16}$ in. (232 × 332 mm.)

TB CCCXXXIV-4

The atmospheric color studies that Turner made during or after his stay in Venice in 1840 broadened and increased the flexibility of his watercolor technique, and the vast quantity of work that he produced as a result of his journeys to Switzerland in 1841–44 demonstrates a very wide range of technical and expressive resource. The devices that he employs in these drawings of the last decade of his life are not in themselves new: the colored pen outlines are to be found in work of the early 1830s; the evanescent washes, as we have seen, were evolved at least by 1819; the color construction clearly observable in this design, with its irradiating segments of umber, yellow and blue (cf. No. 61) follows a principle in use in the early 1820s. But all these features take on a new force in the immensely varied mass of the Swiss drawings. This sheet comes from a roll sketchbook such as Turner almost invariably employed by this date, the *Lausanne* book, now disbound. Ruskin noted the "carriage and four driving down on the left, one postillion only, in the foreign fashion; the cathedral is seen through the trees, and the outline line of the Mont Combin in the distance beyond the lake. The walk in front of us is one of the favourite resorts of the townspeople; a nurse with two children is sketched on the left." (*Ruskin on Pictures*, p. 120.) These details of local life, so carefully observed, play an important role in the many large finished watercolors that Turner made from Swiss studies like this (see Nos. 67 and 70 below).

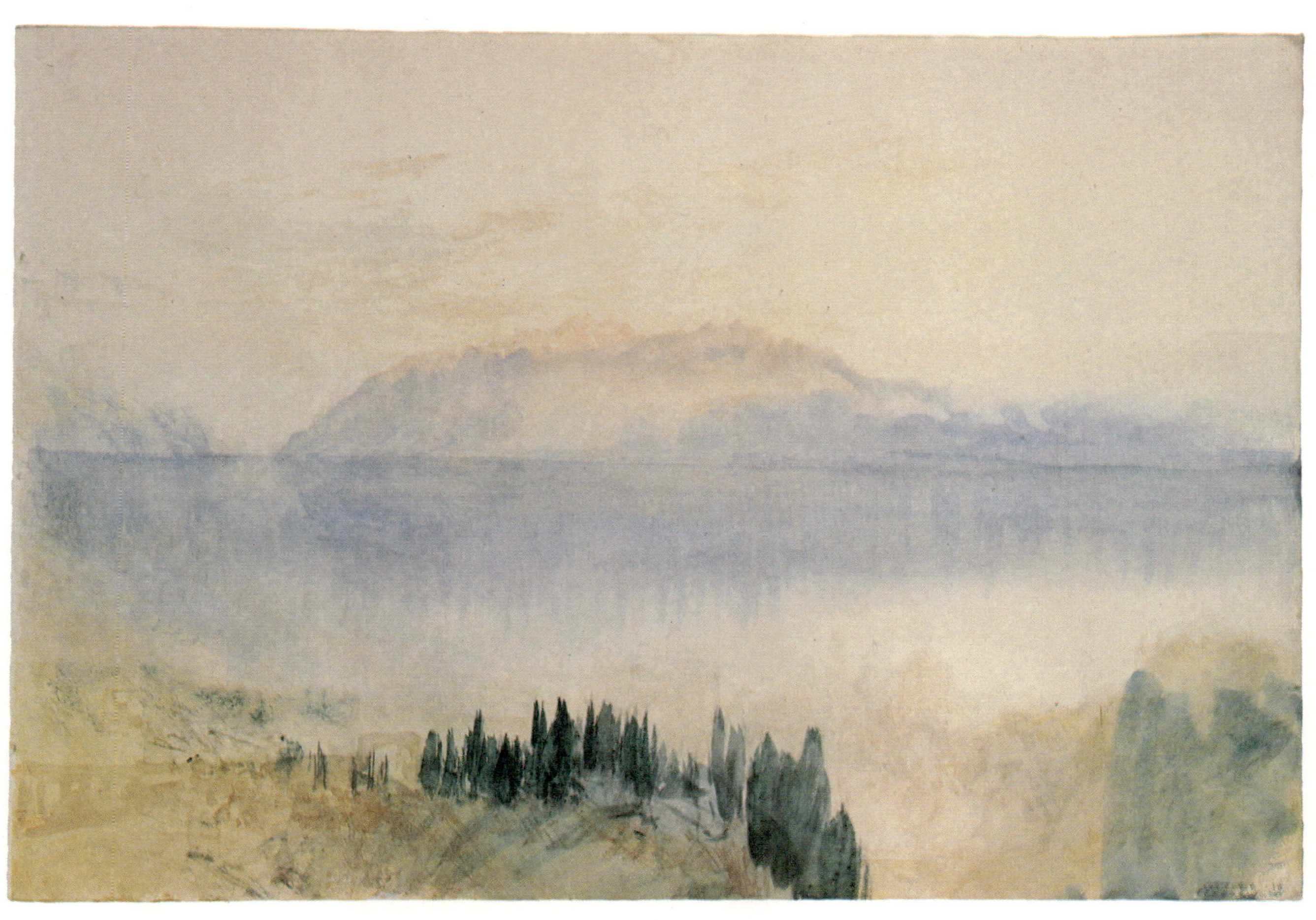

65 **The Lake of Geneva and the Dent d'Oche from Lausanne** 1841

watercolor over pencil, $9\frac{3}{16} \times 13\frac{3}{16}$ in. (233 × 335 mm.)

TB CCCXXXIV-10

A sheet from the *Lausanne* sketchbook, like No. 64, this is a drawing that seems to reflect some of the freshness of color that is to be found in Turner's Venetian studies of 1840, while the concentration of glowing light on the central mountain anticipates the views of the Rigi that he was to make on this tour of Switzerland and afterwards (see No. 68). The frontal simplicity of the composition is also like that of the Rigi subjects, and is one that frequently in Turner's work conveys a mood of tranquil meditation before the grander phenomena of nature in repose.

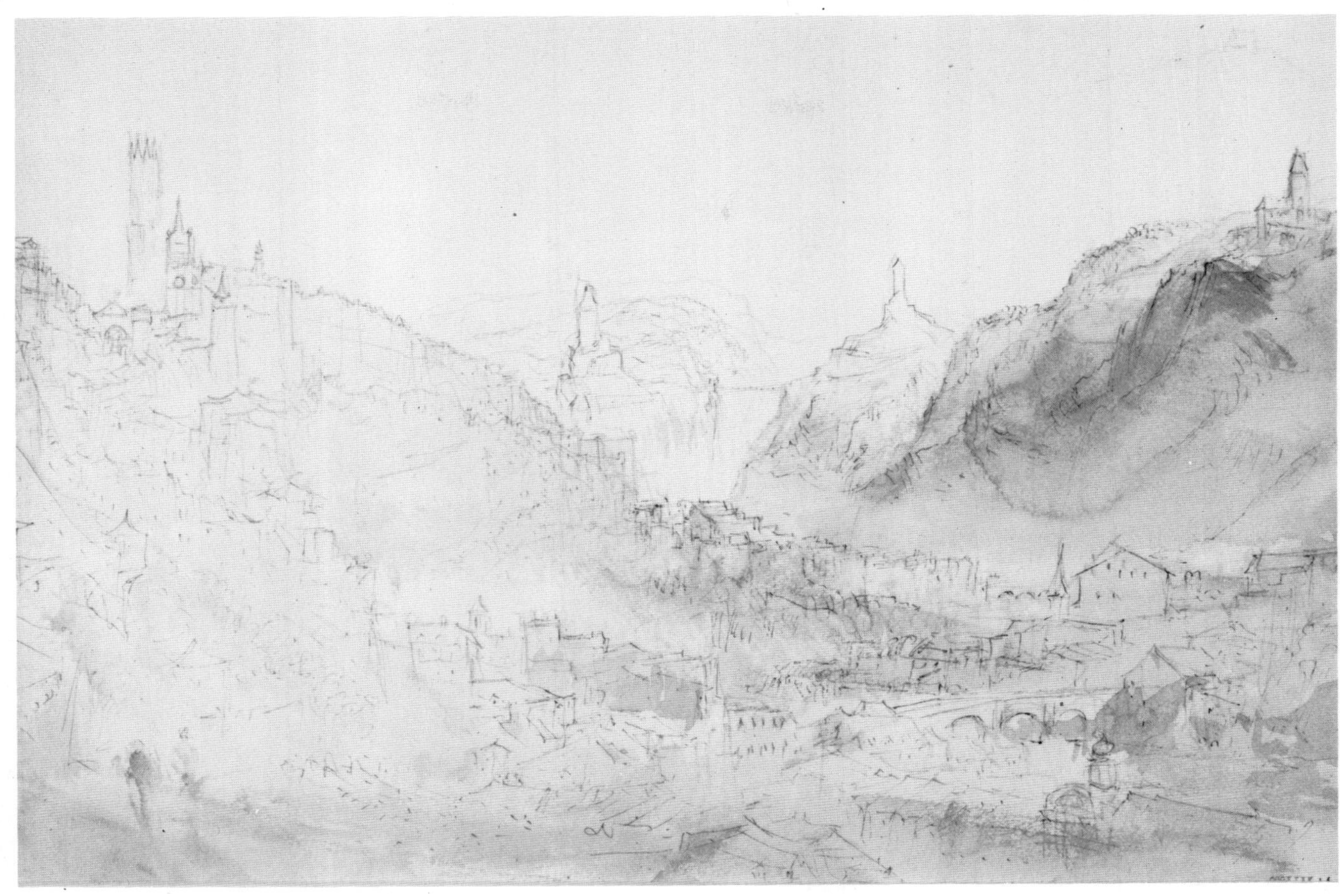

66 **Fribourg: The Descent from the Hôtel de Ville** 1841

watercolor with pen and red ink and red and blue color over pencil

$9\frac{3}{16} \times 13\frac{1}{4}$ in. (233 × 337 mm.)

TB CCCXXXV-14

In his drawings of Fribourg, which fill the *Fribourg* sketchbook, from which this sheet comes, and occur also in the *Fribourg, Lausanne and Geneva* book, TB CCCXXXII, Turner responded in considerable detail to the dramatically sited town with its old houses clustered on the steep slopes of a ravine. As far as we know, he never made a finished watercolor or oil painting of Fribourg, but equipped himself in these studies with a great deal of specific information, in pencil or pen and ink outline, about the disposition of buildings (though always in large groups or general views, not individually). He also recorded his impressions of the grandeur of the setting in broadly-handled watercolor studies. In some cases the two approaches are combined, as here, to present a very complete account of the complex subject, in which, for once, Turner can hardly have found any need to indulge in distortions of scale to achieve "sublime" effects. Again, this composition is rendered coherent by a scheme of blocked colors – in this case, yellow, blue, and pink. Ruskin made the observation, à propos of another drawing which uses the technique of pen outline to delineate architecture: "It is interesting to see how, in putting in the red outlines, Turner always avoids his first pencilled ones." The implication is that, having made an initial record of what he saw, Turner was content thereafter to work with approximations to actuality – the procedure illustrates well his compromise between topography and poetry: a constant shifting and juggling of elements takes place in all his more developed studies (even, sometimes, in pencil sketches made from the motif), and this leads to the "generalized truth" of the finished watercolors. For further comment on the use of pen outline in the late drawings see No. 72.

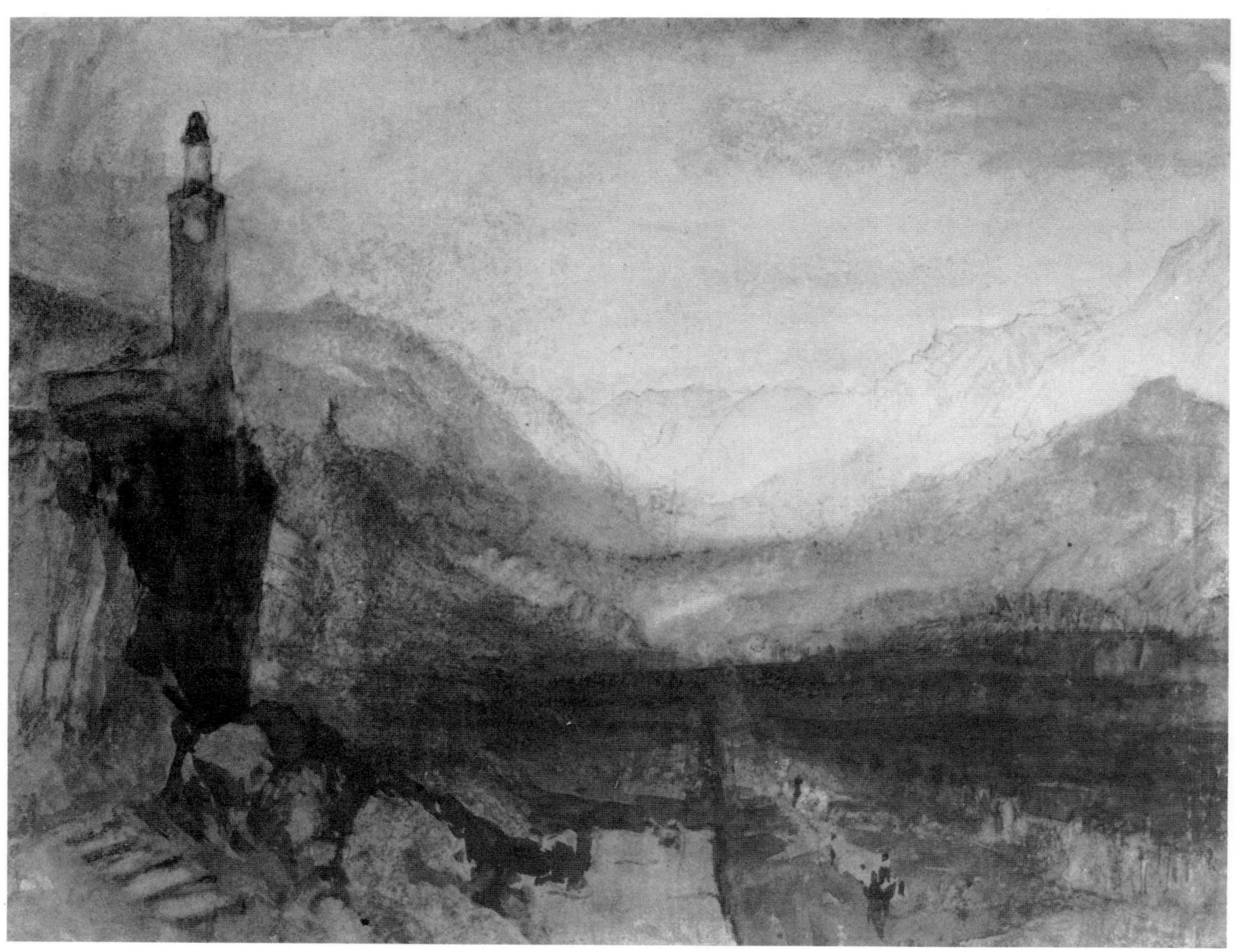

67 **On the Splügen Pass** *c.* 1841

watercolor over traces of pencil, $9\frac{9}{16} \times 12$ in. (242 × 305 mm.)

TB CCCLXIV-277

Ruskin's comment on this study includes the following observation: "We descend to Coire [Chur], and look back from near Ragatz to the higher hills . . . He [Turner] realised the sketch at his own choice with great care." The "realization," one of ten large finished watercolors of Swiss subjects that he made in 1842, is now in a private collection in the USA.[1] Turner had put four of these carefully finished works, together with fifteen roll sketchbook color studies which were offered as "samples," into the hands of his agent, Griffith, with the object of soliciting commissions for finished drawings like the completed *Splügen*. Ruskin, and Turner's companion on a journey that he had made to the Val d'Aosta in 1836, H. A. J. Munro of Novar, were the principal sponsors for this project. Munro purchased the finished *Splügen*, and in a sale of his possessions in 1878 it was catalogued as "Baths of Pfeffers; Ragaz, Pass of Splügen." This suggests that the church on the left of the composition is that of Maienfeld. A recent proposal as to the location of the scene is that it is a view further south on the pass, looking north from Andeer, towards the Via Mala; the foreground is strewn with slabs of stone which may be the product of the granite quarry at Andeer (see Russell and Wilton, *Turner in Switzerland*, p. 109). The point is of minor importance: Turner's design is one of the grandest of his finished watercolors, with a centrifugal plan of great power and airy splendor, analogous to the composition of a very different work of the same period: *Rain, Steam and Speed*,[2] exhibited at the Royal Academy in 1844 (National Gallery, London). The dynamism of its irradiating perspective is, if anything, enhanced in the finished version, where a host of small details give concrete life and set the massive scale of the landscape.

1 Repr. Russell and Wilton, 1976, p. 109.

2 Repr. Herrmann, pl. 175.

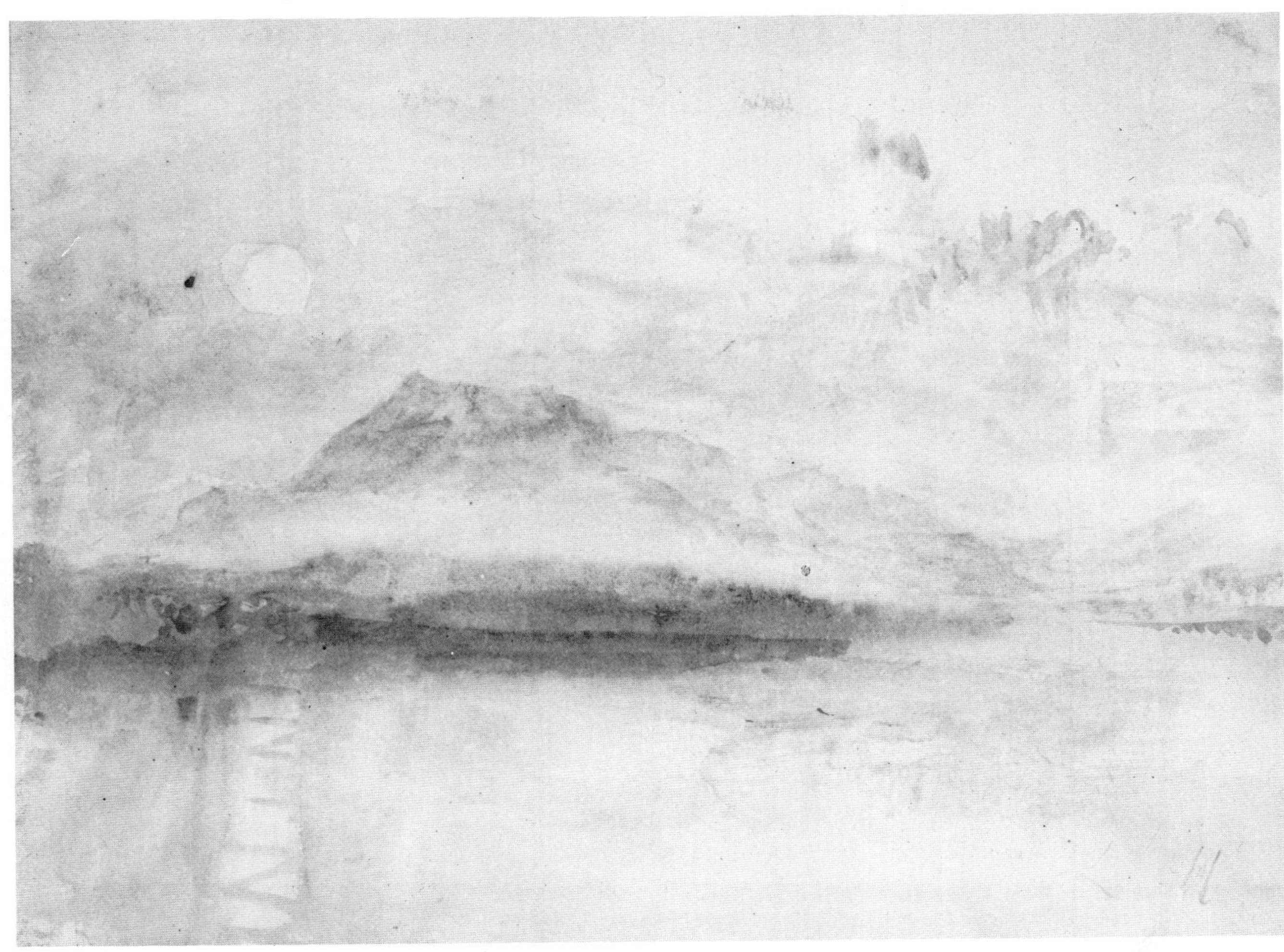

68 **The Rigi: Pink, with a Full Moon** *c.* 1841

watercolor, $10\frac{7}{8} \times 13\frac{5}{8}$ in. (276 × 345 mm.)

inscr. lower right: *L 11*

TB CCCLXIV-192

Three views of the Rigi[1] figure among the ten finished Swiss watercolors made by Turner in 1841–42 (see No. 67), and in addition to the "sample" studies for these he drew a number of informal color sketches of the famous mountain in varying lights, ranging in type from the merest suggestions of tone (e.g. No. 69) to fairly elaborate drawings with much of the quality of finished works. There can be no certainty that they were all done at the same time; indeed, while some definitely precede the finished watercolors of 1842, others occur in a sketchbook (TB CCCXLV) that is watermarked 1844 and must therefore belong to Turner's final visit to Lucerne. This study has something of the bold, rather coarse handling to be found in the sketches in that late book, but it is perhaps more likely to have been done rather earlier. The inscription in the lower right corner indicates that it is one of a series of Lucerne subjects either sketched at the same time or grouped together by the artist for some reason of his own.

1 The three *Rigi* subjects are reproduced in Russell and Wilton, 1976, pp. 86–87, 89, and 90–91.

69 **The Rigi: Pale Gray and Yellow** *c.* 1841

watercolor, $9\frac{13}{16} \times 14\frac{9}{16}$in. (249 × 370 mm.)

inscr. below: *Stadtz* and, lower right: *L 18*

TB CCCLXIV-196

As the number inscribed by Turner on the sheet shows, this drawing belongs to the same group of "Lucerne" drawings as No. 68. It is perhaps the most ethereal of all Turner's evocations of the Rigi, reminiscent of the misty views that he had made in Venice, probably shortly before. It is not, of course, on that account to be considered an "abstraction:" it is a vivid presentation of a natural phenomenon that is clearly recognizable and readily understood; though few landscape artists have chosen to render such effects heightened to so intense a degree by poetic sensitivity. Turner's consciousness of the basic topographical facts on which his art as a watercolorist had always been built is well suggested by his note of the name *Stadtz* at the bottom of the page, which presumably refers to the town of Stanz, situated below the Burgenstock on the southern side of Lake Lucerne, beyond the Rigi to its right.

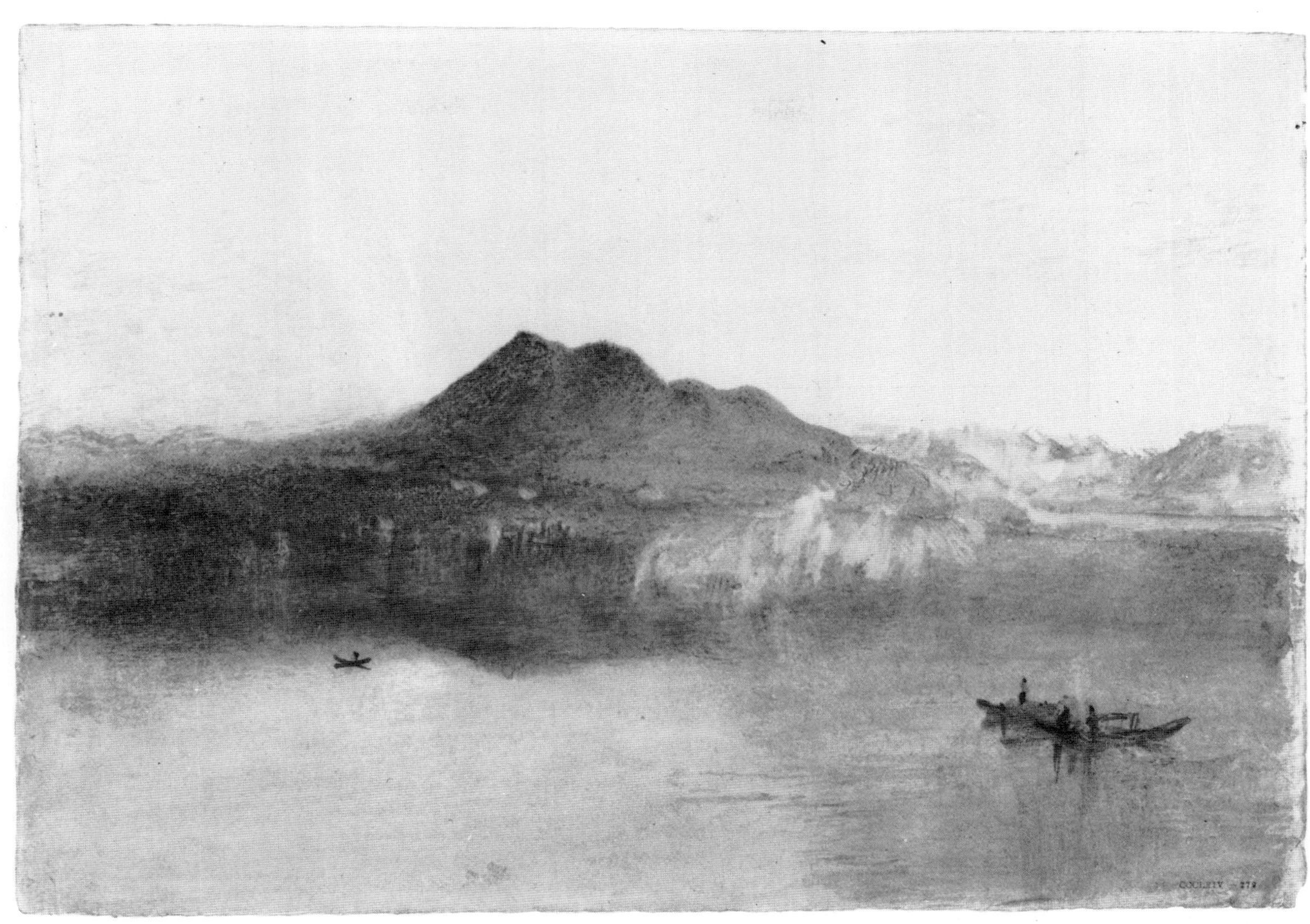

70 **Study for "The Dark Rigi"** *c.* 1841

watercolor, $9\frac{1}{16} \times 12\frac{11}{16}$ in. (230 × 322 mm.)

inscr. *verso*: *J. A. Munro Esq 31*

TB CCCLXIV-279

The inscription on the back of this sheet indicates that the subject was selected by Turner's friend and patron Munro of Novar as one of five that the artist was to make for him from the "samples" presented to Griffith in the winter of 1841–42 (see the *Pass of Splügen*, No. 67). The composition became known as *The Dark Rigi*, a kind of companion to two other views of the mountain, the *Blue Rigi* and the *Red Rigi* (now in a private collection, U.K., and the National Gallery of Victoria, Melbourne, respectively). Munro, however, did not acquire the *Blue Rigi*. Ruskin described the finished *Dark Rigi* as "Mont Righi seen from the window of his [Turner's] inn, 'La Cygne,' in the dawn of a lovely summer's morning; a fragment of fantastic mist hanging between us and the hill." The main elements of this ecstatic vision of tranquility are already present in Turner's study, which has been considerably worked up with delicate hatching, in the manner of a finished watercolor, to achieve the solidity and at the same time the elusive coloration of the mountain.

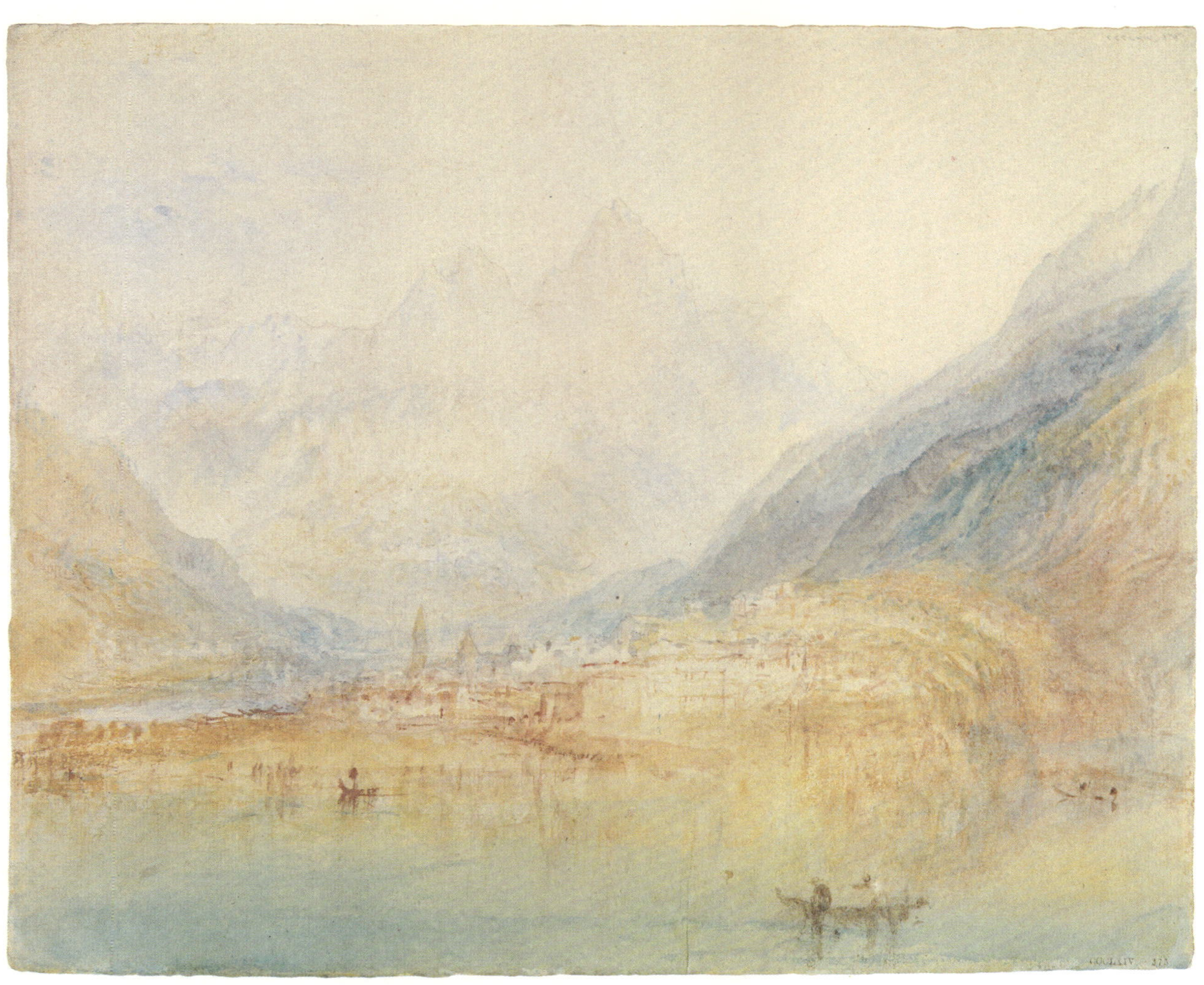

71 **Brunnen and the Mythen from Lake Lucerne** ?1844

pencil and watercolor, $9\frac{7}{16} \times 11\frac{1}{2}$ in. (240 × 293 mm.)

TB CCCLXIV-375

Griffith failed to find all ten of the customers that Turner had asked for in 1842 (see No. 67), but the artist was not deflected from his intention by lack of public interest: he made all ten finished watercolors and gave one of them to Griffith in lieu of commission; in the following year he made six more, all acquired by Ruskin and Munro. No circumstances could more effectually demolish the claim, often put forward, that Turner's finished watercolors were done as a mere sop to contemporary taste, and that he expressed himself primarily through his preliminary or exploratory studies. The great finished Swiss watercolors of these years rank among Turner's most impassioned and moving works; they are technically as complex and painstaking as anything he had ever produced in the medium, and their union of the detail of ordinary life with the majestic sweeps of "Sublime" nature sums up the motive force behind a large proportion of his whole output. The immense landscapes of Switzerland were particularly well suited to his love of vastness, and especially of the vastness of the open air, in which light undergoes innumerable modifications within the scope of a single *coup d'oeil*. After his final visit of 1844, Turner made yet another set of finished drawings, presumably based on notes taken in that year, though quite possibly using material collected on earlier tours. This sheet was one of the "sample" studies for that group; Ruskin called it "very elaborate and beautiful, the dark slope of the hills on the right especially. Note the value," he added, "of the little violet touch of light behind their central darkest ridge." The study prompted Ruskin to commission a finished watercolor of the subject. This was executed in 1845;[1] but "in the sketch there were no ugly hotels; in the drawing he put them in and spoiled his subject." Ruskin accordingly gave the finished *Brunnen* to Munro, in exchange for another of the 1845 set; it is now in the Clark Institute, Williamstown, Mass.

1 Repr. Russell and Wilton, 1976, p. 93.

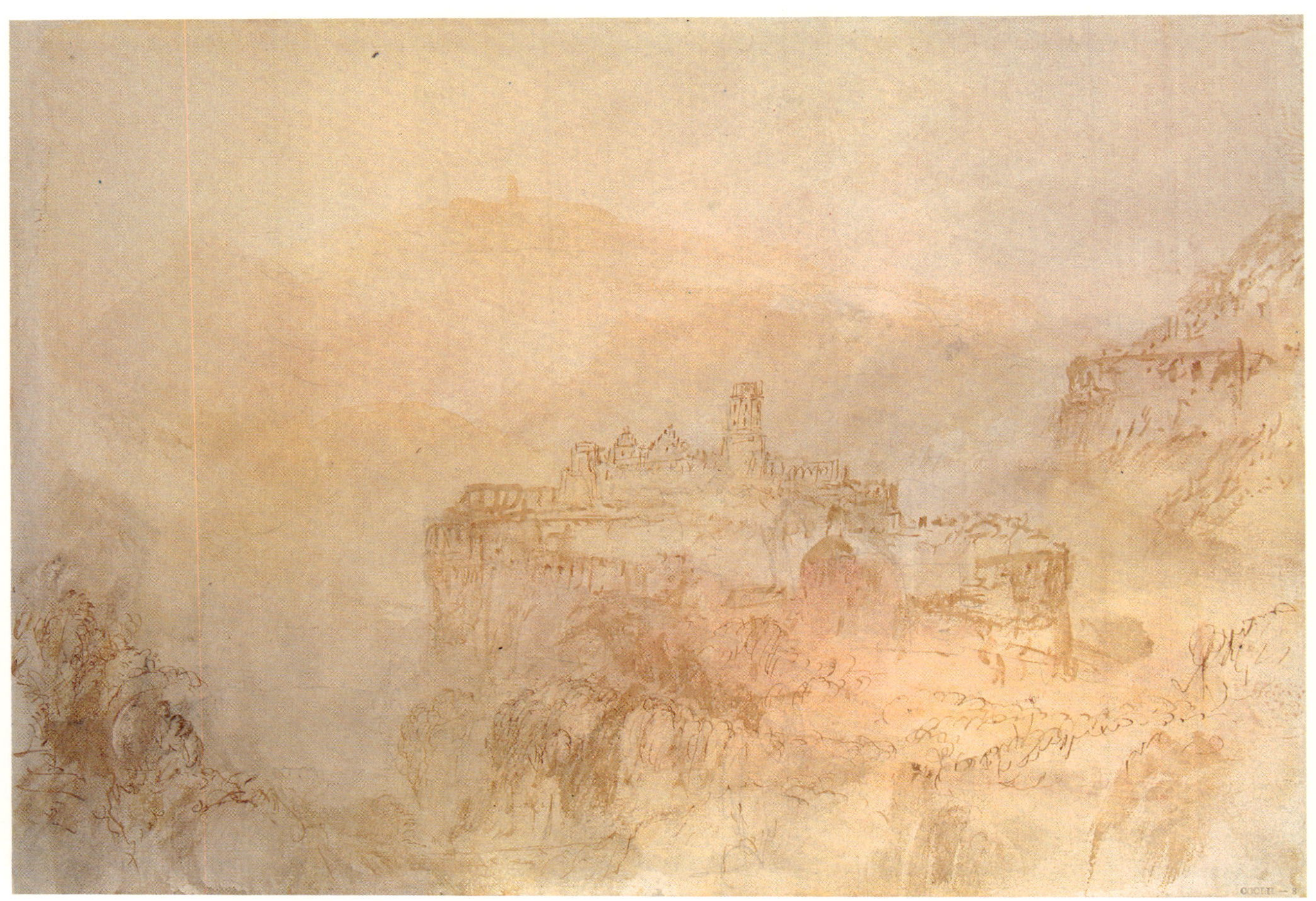

72 **Heidelberg: The Castle Seen from Above** 1844

pencil and watercolor with some pen, 9 × 12⅞ in. (229 × 328 mm.)

TB CCCLII-8

This is a sheet from a sketchbook (*Heidelberg*) in which Turner made many studies of the city, rather as he had done of Fribourg in 1841 (see No. 66), and using a similar technique, especially in the outlining of detail with a pen dipped in the principal colors of the design, by which means he indicates broad patterns of color while maintaining the brilliant luminosity of the whole subject. Both Heidelberg and Fribourg, with their combination of ancient, clustered buildings and dramatic natural setting, seem to have prompted similar responses from Turner, but at this later date the suggestion of the disintegration of forms in light is more marked. He executed one large oil painting of Heidelberg,[1] (Tate Gallery TB 518), in which some of his watercolor technique is applied to the creation of airy, shining spaces, the forms built up on a white ground. It is characteristic of the "cross-fertilization" that took place between the two media during the last decade or so of the artist's life (see also No. 62). He also made a number of finished watercolors of Heidelberg from the river, at different dates between about 1838 and 1850; the latest and grandest of them[2] (Edinburgh, National Gallery of Scotland) seems to be one of the last finished watercolors that he did (see Russell and Wilton, *Turner in Switzerland*, p. 140).

1 Repr. Herrmann, 1975, pl. 161.

2 The last of Turner's *Heidelberg* watercolors, probably executed about 1850, is reproduced (with a date of *c.* 1840) in Herrmann, 1975, pl. 149.

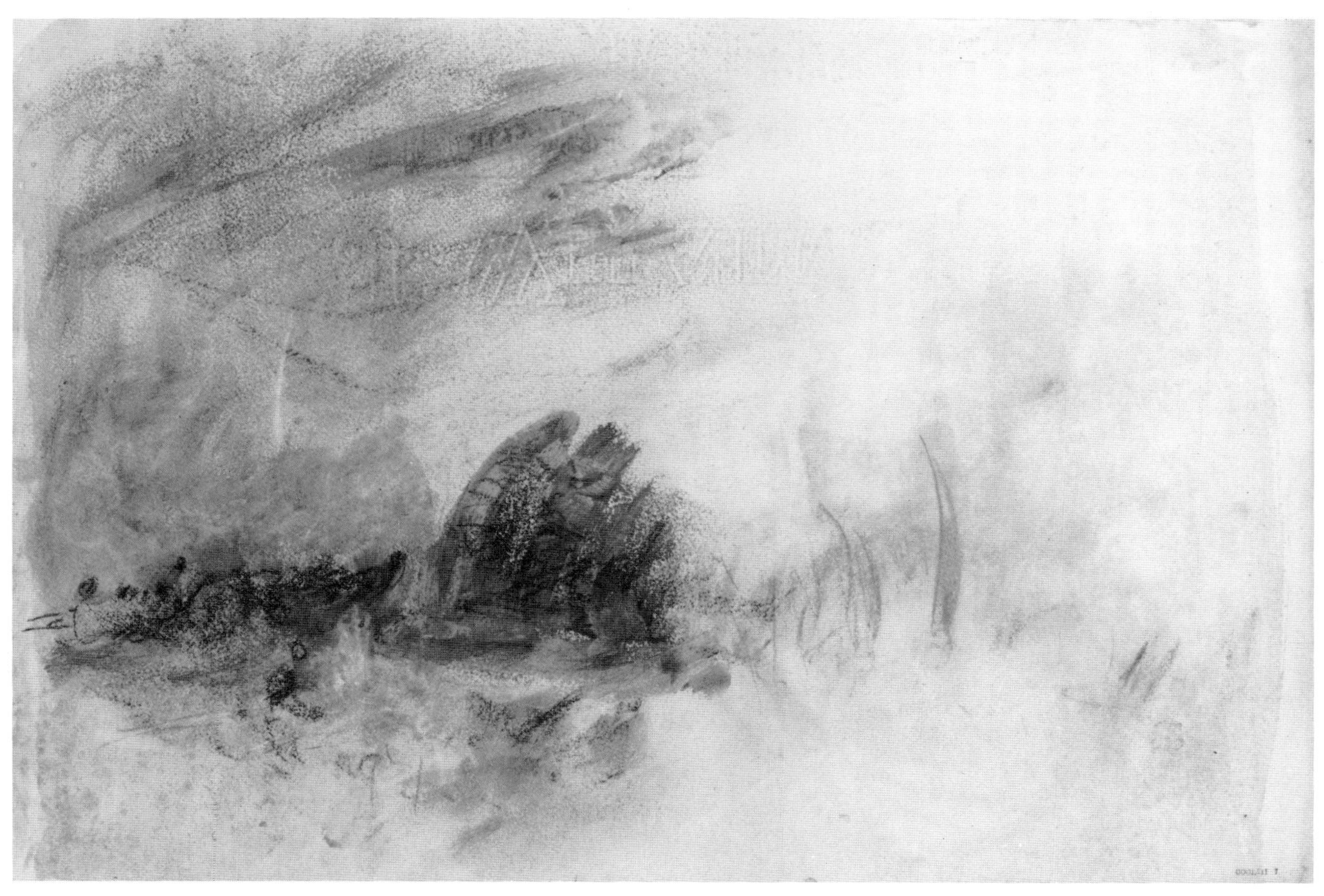

73 **Whalers Boiling Blubber** *c.* 1845

watercolor, bodycolor and colored chalks, $8\frac{11}{16} \times 13\frac{1}{8}$ in. (221 × 332 mm.)

TB CCCLIII-7

Turner showed four pictures with whaling subjects at the Royal Academy in 1845 and 1846. One of these is now in the Metropolitan Museum, New York. Another, exhibited at the Royal Academy in 1846 (494), shows a scene similar to this drawing and was entitled *Whalers (Boiling Blubber) Entangled in Flaw Ice, Endeavouring to Extricate Themselves*[1] (Tate Gallery TB 547). They appear to have been inspired by the publication (in 1839) of Thomas Beale's *The Natural History of the Sperm Whale*, but there are a number of watercolor studies of whaling scenes which suggest that Turner actually saw a whale at about the time of his last crossing to the Continent in 1845, when he visited the north French coast. For whatever reason, he took up the idea, not only in the watercolor sketches and oil paintings just mentioned, but also in a series of studies in an unusual combination of media, of which this is an example. The grand effect of firelight in darkness is characteristic of his lifelong search for "Sublime" pictorial drama, retained from the days of his earliest work in oil and continued in late paintings such as the *Burning of the Houses of Parliament* (see No. 47), *Keelmen Heaving in Coals by Night*[2] (1835; National Gallery, Washington) and *Peace: Burial at Sea* (1842; Tate Gallery TB 528).

1 The Metropolitan *Whalers* is Butlin and Joll, 1977, No. 415; *Whalers (Boiling Blubber)* . . . is repr. RA 1974–75, No. 524, p. 149.

2 Repr. Herrmann, 1975, pl. 143.

Selected Bibliography

Selected Bibliography

Thornbury, Walter. *The Life of J. M. W. Turner, R.A.* 2 vols. London: Jurst and Blackett, 1862.

Rawlinson, W. G. *Turner's Liber Studiorum, A Description and a Catalogue.* London: Macmillan and Co., 1878.

Ruskin, John. *Ruskin on Pictures.* Edited by E. T. Cook, 1902.

Rawlinson, W. G. *The Engraved Work of J. M. W. Turner, R.A.* 2 vols. London: Macmillan and Co., 1908–13.

Finberg, A. J. *A Complete Inventory of the Drawings of the Turner Bequest.* 2 vols. London: Printed for H.M. Stationery Office by Darling & Son, Ltd., 1909.

———. *Turner's Sketches and Drawings.* 1910. Reprint with introduction by Lawrence Gowing. New York: Schocken Books, 1968.

———. *The Life of J. M. W. Turner, R.A.*, 1939. 2d ed., rev. and with a supplement by Hilda F. Finberg. Oxford: The Clarendon Press, 1961.

Butlin, Martin. *Turner Watercolours.* London: Barrie and Rockliff, 1962.

Rothenstein, John and Butlin, Martin. *Turner.* New York: G. Braziller, 1964.

Gowing, Lawrence. *Turner: Imagination and Reality.* New York: Distributed by Doubleday, 1966.

Lindsay, Jack. *J. M. W. Turner: His Life and Work; A Critical Biography.* Greenwich, Conn.: New York Graphic Society, 1966.

Herrmann, Luke. *Ruskin and Turner.* New York: F. A. Praeger, 1969.

Gage, John. *Colour in Turner; Poetry and Truth.* London: Studio Vista, 1969.

Reynolds, Graham. *Turner.* London: Thames & Hudson, 1969.

———. "Turner at East Cowes Castle." *Victoria and Albert Museum Yearbook*, vol. 1, 1969, pp. 67–79.

George, Hardy. "Turner in Venice." *Art Quarterly*, vol. 53, 1971, pp. 84–87.

Wilkinson, Gerald. *Turner's Early Sketchbooks.* London: Barrie and Jenkins, 1972.

Butlin, Martin; Gage, John; and Wilton, Andrew. *Turner, 1775–1851.* Catalogue of a Bicentenary exhibition at Burlington House. London 1974.

Wilkinson, Gerald. *The Sketches of Turner, R.A., 1802–20: Genius of the Romantic.* London: Barrie and Jenkins, 1974.

Cormack, Malcolm. *J. M. W. Turner, R.A. 1775–1851: A Catalogue of Drawings and Watercolours in the Fitzwilliam Museum.* Cambridge, 1975.

Wilkinson, Gerald. *Turner's Colour Sketches, 1820–34*. London: Barrie and Jenkins, 1975.

Goldyne, Joseph R. *J. M. W. Turner, Works on Paper from American Collections*. Berkeley, University Art Museum, 1975.

Herrmann, Luke. *Turner, Paintings, Watercolours, Prints and Drawings*. London: Phaidon, 1975.

Wilton, Andrew. *Turner in the British Museum*. London: Published for the Trustees of the British Museum by British Museum Publications, 1975.

Russell, John, and Wilton, Andrew. *Turner in Switzerland*. Zurich, 1976.

Walker, John. *Joseph Mallord William Turner*. New York: Harry N. Abrams, Inc., 1976.

Butlin, Martin, and Joll, Evelyn. *Catalogue of Turner's Paintings*. Forthcoming, Autumn 1977.

Abbreviations Used in Catalogue

BM, 1975 – Wilton, Andrew. *Turner in the British Museum*. London: Published for the Trustees of the British Museum by British Museum Publications, 1975.

R – Rawlinson, W. G. *The Engraved Work of J. M. W. Turner, R.A.* 2 vols. London: Macmillan and Co., 1908–13.

RA, 1974–75 – *Turner 1775–1851*. Bicentenary exhibition at the Royal Academy, 16 Nov. 1974–2 March, 1975. London: Tate Gallery Publications, 1974.

TB – Turner Bequest references from Finberg, A. J. *A Complete Inventory of the Drawings of the Turner Bequest*. 2 vols. London: Printed for H.M. Stationery Office by Darling & Son, Ltd., 1909.